Buffalo Soldiers

The 92nd Infantry Division and Reinforcements in World War II, 1942-1945

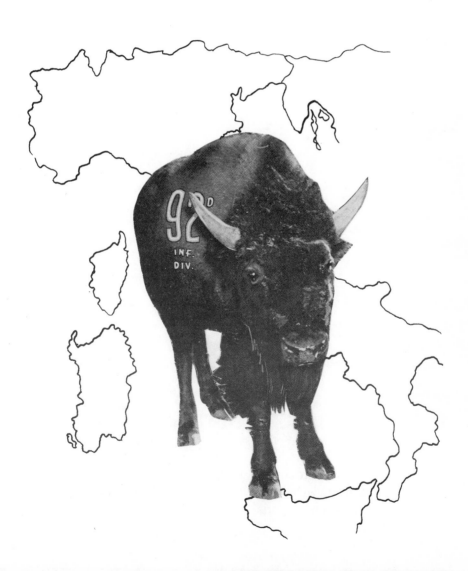

All maps are courtesy of the U.S. Army. Cartoons were drawn by enlisted personnel to illustrate G-3 Operations Reports.

Buffalo Soldiers

The 92nd Infantry Division and Reinforcements in World War II, 1942-1945

by
Thomas St. John Arnold, OBE
Colonel, United States Army (Retired)

*To Winfield Massie
with best wishes

Thomas St John Arnold*

Sunflower University Press®
1531 Yuma (Box 1009), Manhattan, Kansas 66502-4228 USA

ISBN 0-89745-127-9

Edited by Ann Warren

Layout by Lori L. Daniel

To the more than 5,000. . . .

Black, White, Japanese-American, British, Indian, and Italian soldiers who fell in combat while fighting with the 92nd Infantry Division in Italy during the period 24 August 1944 to 2 May 1945.

15 October 1989

Contents

Foreword

I and other men of the 442nd Infantry Regimental Combat Team held the highest respect for the 92nd Division. In addition to being comrades in arms against Nazism, we were also fighting another battle — one against racism and bigotry. Sad to say, this battle goes on today.

I have a special, personal memory of the 92nd. In the hours after I was wounded and doctors were treating me at the field hospital, I remember a nurse showing me a bottle of blood. It had a name on it — Thomas Jefferson Smith, 92nd Division — and while they were rigging it for transfusion into my left arm, I realized that fighting men did more than fight, that they cared enough about each other and the men assigned to their sector to donate their blood for the time when somebody would need it to sustain life. I was to have 17 transfusions in that first week alone. I am very, very grateful for it, and perhaps this is a fitting time to extend my thanks to every man in the 92nd Division who donated blood that helped save my life.

Daniel K. Inouye
United States Senator

FORECAST

Partly cloudy with 20 percent chance of showers and thunderstorms. South and southwest wind near 10 mph. High today 95. Low early Tuesday 74.

YESTERDAY'S TEMPERATURES
(airport readings)

High — 93 degrees at 3 p.m.
(Record — 100 degrees in 1986)
Low — 72 degrees at 7 a.m.
(Record — 67 degrees in 1938)
Galveston surf .... 88 degrees

RAINFALL
(airport reading, inches to 4 p.m.)

Yesterday — .06

This month — .06	Normal — .20
This year — 38.05	Normal — 25.66

YESTERDAY'S HUMIDITIES
(airport readings, percentages)

12:01 a.m. —100	6 a.m. —100
12:01 p.m. —66	6 p.m. —68

POLLEN

	Lt.	Med.	Hvy.
MOLD SPORE:	☐	☑	☐
GRASS POLLEN:	☑	☐	☐
RAGWEED:	☐	☐	☐
TREE POLLEN:	☐	☐	☐

POLLUTION

Friday's Count: 44

300-500	☐	Hazardous
200-299	☐	Very Poor
101-199	☐	Poor
51-100	☐	Moderate
0-50	☑	Good

W

Sa
Franc
74/

TEMPERATURES

STATE	Yesterday Hi/Lo-Prec	Today Hi/Lo-Outlook	Tomorrow Hi/Lo-Outlook
Abilene	92/69	95/73 ptcldy	94/72 ptcldy
Amarillo	93/65	89/63 ptcldy	90/62 ptcldy
Austin	96/75	98/76 ptcldy	96/75 ptcldy
Beaumont	92/72	92/74 tstorms	93/76 ptcldy
Brownsville	96/76	96/77 ptcldy	95/75 ptcldy
Bryan-Coll. St.	94/71	94/73 ptcldy	96/74 ptcldy
Corpus Christi	94/74	94/76 ptcldy	95/75 ptcldy
Dallas Ft Worth	96/70-0.08	96/73 ptcldy	94/72 ptcldy
Del Rio	93/75	100/74 ptcldy	101/74 ptcldy
El Paso	91/64	95/68 ptcldy	96/67 ptcldy
Galveston	86/76-0.44	90/76 ptcldy	89/74 ptcldy
Laredo	99/77	101/75 ptcldy	102/75 ptcldy
Lubbock	95/67	90/65 ptcldy	89/64 ptcldy

h-deserved recognition

national expansion. At the time, the Army didn't have enough white soldiers to fill all of the necessary units, so it created the first permanent all-black units — the 9th and 10th Cavalry.

The units were made up of mostly newly freed slaves and they were normally commanded by white officers.

The regiments initially were sent out West, where they developed into distinguished fighting forces. And it was out on the plains, while fighting Indians, that the units became known as the Buffalo Soldiers. The Indians, whom the soldiers fought and killed, said the troops' woolly heads of hair reminded them of the buffalo they regarded so highly.

Sadly, while fighting for their country, the black soldiers helped bring about the capitulation of the Indians on the frontier. They also helped to introduce the rule of law along the border with Mexico where they fought Pancho Villa.

When the units were formed, whites still looked on Negroes with suspicion. The regiments were treated harshly, but their battle-worthiness wasn't questioned after the first few firefights.

Still, they were barred from the Fort Leavenworth parade field, were paid less than whites, and many officers, including Gen. George Custer, refused to serve with them. Yet the Buffalo Soldiers persevered. They reportedly captured — but lost — Pancho Villa while he was raiding Texas towns, and they protected pioneer settlements from the Dakotas to the land of the Apache. Their desertion rate was low, and, from 1867 to 1898, they won 20 Medals of Honor. They also fought alongside Teddy Roosevelt in Cuba during the Spanish-American War.

Cmdr. Philpot says they saved Roosevelt's reputation in the battle for Kettle Hill and were instrumental in securing a way for the fabled Rough Riders to take San Juan Hill and guarantee victory.

Roosevelt was so grateful that he was said to have told the blacks that they could "drink out of my canteen" any time. But Philpot notes that later the rhetoric changed. The Navy commander says Roosevelt was told that he could not praise black troops and become president, so he accused them of some combat dereliction. Philpot believes the false accusations have lived on to the present.

And although the units remained all-black until the early 1950s, they have been largely relegated — probably because they were black — to the barely remembered category of military lore.

It's a shame this history is so sketchy. But it's good to see it memorialized.

Buffalo Soldiers get muc

Robert C. Newberry

I T DID MY HEART good to see the Army's 9th and 10th Cavalry — the Buffalo Soldiers — finally get some of the recognition they so richly deserve. A monument has been built honoring the black troops' role in settling the West and in fighting foreign battles from the Spanish-American War to the Korean War.

The monument, erected at Fort Leavenworth, Kan., where the units were first organized, is a large bronze statue of a horse-mounted black soldier.

It was dedicated last week to mark the 126th anniversary of the formation of the 9th and 10th Cavalry. The statue's unveiling by Chairman of the Joint Chiefs of Staff Gen. Colin Powell capped a 10-year struggle started by Powell himself.

Powell, who is also black, conceived the idea in 1982 while stationed at Fort Leavenworth. He discovered that the only recognition of the 9th and 10th was a pair of alleyways. He said he thought the fort could do better than that.

But before Powell could do much, he was transferred to another post. His idea languished. A little money for a memorial was raised, but nothing even came of it.

Then Navy Cmdr. Carlton Philpot arrived in 1989 to work as an instructor at the Army Command and General Staff School. Although trained to ride ships-

rather than horses, Philpot saw some merit in what Powell wanted to do. He got 20 volunteers, set a goal of $900,000, and hired black sculptor Eddie Dixon of Lubbock to do the 12-foot statue.

Philpot directed the entire project. "I am a black man," he said, "I went to a black college, and I never heard of the Buffalo Soldiers. They are just not in the history books. That's why this memorial is important. We want to remind the nation of the role black people — soldiers — have played." Good for him.

The Buffalo Soldier statue is built on a scenic site near a lake. It will be maintained by the U.S. Army; otherwise, there has been no public expense. The volunteers raised $860,000 — in private funds — but $40,000 is still needed.

The two regiments were formed right after the Civil War in 1866 when the United States reorganized its military to meet the demands of Reconstruction and

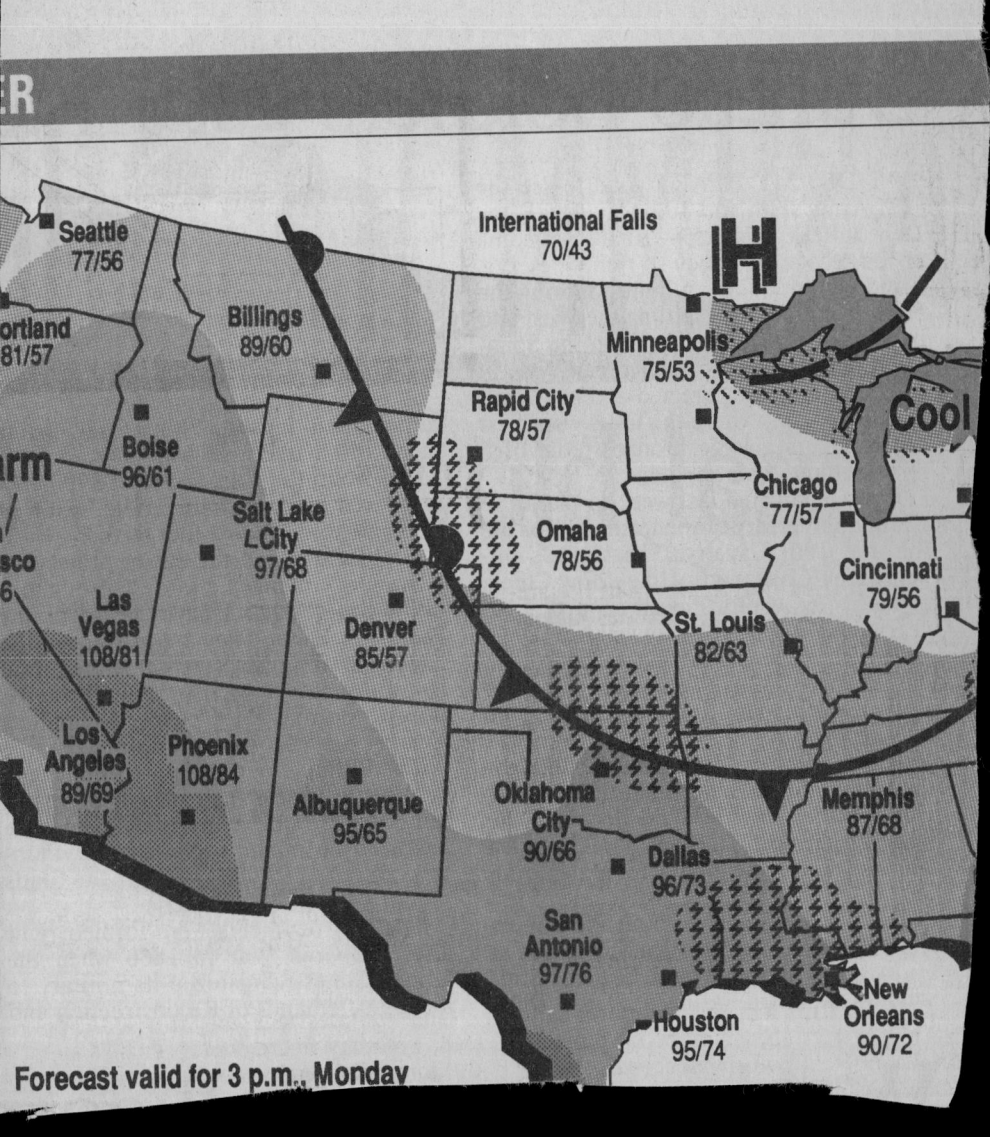

ER

Seattle
77/56

Portland
81/57

Billings
89/60

International Falls
70/43

H

Minneapolis
75/53

Rapid City
78/57

Cool

arm

Boise
96/61

Salt Lake
L.City
97/68

Chicago
77/57

sco
6

Las
Vegas
108/81

Omaha
78/56

Denver
85/57

St. Louis
82/63

Cincinnati
79/56

Los
Angeles
89/69

Phoenix
108/84

Albuquerque
95/65

Oklahoma
City
90/66

Dallas
96/73

Memphis
87/68

San
Antonio
97/76

Houston
95/74

New
Orleans
90/72

Forecast valid for 3 p.m., Monday

Introduction

This is the story of a unique military force. The 92nd Infantry division was not only the only black division to fight in World War II as a division, but will also undoubtedly be the last black division the United States will ever put into the field. When reinforced by the attachment of many United States, British, and Italian troop units, it became integrated at regimental and unit level as well as a combined Allied force. It was the largest division the United States put into the field in World War II.

Blacks have fought in all of America's wars from the Boston Massacre, on 5 March 1770, to the present. Following the Revolutionary War, Washington's Army was disbanded, and the United States was left with only a token force to guard its vital installations. Gen. Andrew Jackson, whose Army for a time was not recognized by the federal government, arrived at the Battle of New Orleans with two black battalions. At the outset of the Civil War, the United States was seriously unprepared. It was forced to rely on state militia which, initially, were untrained and poorly organized. The 54th and 55th Massachusetts Infantry Regiments were among the 145 Infantry, 7 Cavalry, 12 Heavy Artillery, and 1 Light Artillery black regiments of militia included in the Union Forces.

It was not until after the Civil War that black organizations were included in the Regular Army of the United States. They were the 24th and 25th Infantry Regiments and the 9th and 10th Cavalry Regiments. The 9th Cavalry Regiment was employed in Texas. The 10th Cavalry was stationed at Fort Riley, Kansas, and patrolled out of Fort Harkers. Its commanding officer encouraged his troopers to wear anything comfortable while on patrol; thus, to protect themselves against the rigors of winter weather, the troopers wore overcoats made of buffalo hides.

The Plains Indians called the troopers "Buffalo Soldiers" because the tightly curled hair of the black men and their buffalo skin coats reminded the Indians of the buffalo. The troopers liked the term "Buffalo Soldiers" since the buffalo was revered. The 9th and 10th Cavalry Regiments were active in protecting small settler communities and mail stations, and in escorting wagon trains and stagecoaches. They made up 40 percent of the cavalry engaged in the Indian Campaigns. Later, all four black regiments were sent to Cuba in the Spanish-American War. Theodore Roosevelt's Rough Riders would not have survived the Battle of San Juan Hill if the 10th Cavalry and the 24th Infantry Regiments had not come to their rescue. In 1916, when Mexican Gen. Pancho Villa crossed the border and raided in New Mexico, the 10th Cavalry and 24th and 25th Infantry Regiments were sent to the border to assist Brig. Gen. John J. Pershing in his pursuit.

As the threat of war in Europe developed, the United States was once again caught seriously unprepared to meet its military commitments. Despite advance warning and some advance preparation during 1916, a year passed between the declaration of war and the entry of an American division into battle. Military preparations for participation in World War I envisioned the creation of two black divisions in the Army. However, only the 92nd Division was actually formed, with an initial strength of approximately 25,000 black enlisted men and about 1,000 white and black officers. Small unit training was conducted at seven camps. It was first assembled as a division at Camp Upton, New York, and subsequently moved to Hoboken, New Jersey, and then to France in June 1918. Its initial entry into action was on a relatively quiet sector of St. Kie in the Vosges Mountains. Following this, it was moved to the Argonne in time for the Meuse-Argonne offensive which began on 24 September 1918. Later, the division had successes in the Marbache Sector and Woevre Plain operations in October and November 1918. Following the Armistice, the Division returned to the United States in mid-December 1918 and was demobilized in February and March 1919. The 369th Infantry Regiment was first used for construction and guard duty, and was later trained by and fought under French command. It was to have become part of the 93rd Division.

Even though the Germans accepted virtually all of the terms that the Allied powers had drafted, the Armistice of November 1918 was not an unconditional surrender. It was apparent that both the British and American governments were reluctant to involve their armies in a further advance into Germany. Not so apparent was the Germans' desire for time to rebuild their army and industrial machine. The great American army of nearly two million was out of a job. Demobilization was the order of the day. By 1936, the Army had been reduced to 125,000 men and officers with only one skeleton division head-quarters and scattered battalion and regimental units in the U.S. Its espionage capability had been destroyed when its cryptograph section, known as "The

American Black Chamber," was closed on 31 October 1929; President Herbert Hoover had said that "Gentlemen do not read each other's mail."[1]

Following World War I, Japanese militarists gradually gained control of their government. Their conquest of all of Manchuria, destruction of the U.S. gunboat *Panay*, and invasion of North China received little response. Meanwhile, Benito Mussolini founded the Fascist Party in 1919 and became Dictator of Italy in 1922. In 1935-1936, in defiance of the League of Nations, Italian troops invaded and conquered Ethiopia. The League of Nations attempted to cut off trade with Italy, but otherwise did nothing to prevent Mussolini's aggressive conquest.

During the political confusion after World War I, Adolf Hitler's National Socialist German Worker's Party (Nazi) came to power, and Hitler became Germany's dictator in 1934. Under his direction, Germany reoccupied the Rhineland and Saar regions in violation of the Treaty of Versailles. In his *Mein Kampf*, Hitler outlined his plan to conquer much of Europe, territories lost in World War I, part of Austria, Czechoslovakia, and the Soviet Union. Little or nothing was undertaken by the Western powers to prevent his expansionism until he invaded Poland.

As the United States rushed to rearm itself in 1939, certain cherished national fallacies hampered its efforts. Since Bunker Hill, congressmen as well as schoolchildren had accepted the concept that the patriot, armed with little more than the righteousness of his cause, could quickly take his place behind the country's breastwork or even man a foreign trench. Forgetting the bitter experiences of the Civil War and World War I, many American leaders opposed military training and relied on a simple danger cry to fill the ranks of the Regular Army and the National Guard.

From 3 to 30 August 1940, the largest peacetime maneuver ever held by the United States to that date was conducted in the Plattsburg-Watertown area in northern New York. Approximately 87,000 men and officers of the Regular Army, National Guard, and Organized Reserve participated. Many trucks carried signs stating, "This is a tank." Stove pipes were used for mortars, and beer cans simulated ammunition. Hitler's military attache, observing the maneuver, reported to him that the United States was too divided and too poorly prepared to fight a war.

An alliance of Germany and Italy (and later Japan), known as the Axis, was formed in 1936. On 7 December 1941, Japan attempted to eliminate U.S. combat capability by destroying its Pacific Fleet, then in port at Pearl Harbor, and the Army Air Corps at Clark Field in the Philippines. Following the Japanese attack against the U.S. Naval Base at Pearl Harbor, it was evident that the United States could not fight a war both in the Pacific and in Europe with equal power in both theaters. Because the Japanese had struck first, to many it appeared that they were more dangerous. However, President Roosevelt and

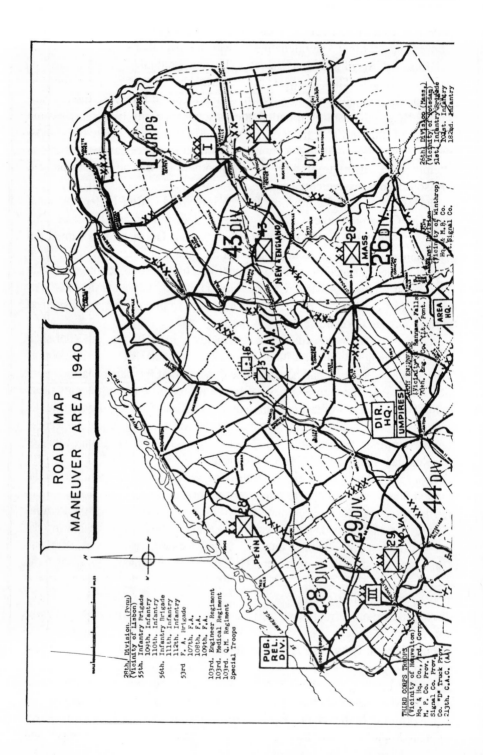

ROAD MAP
MANEUVER AREA 1940

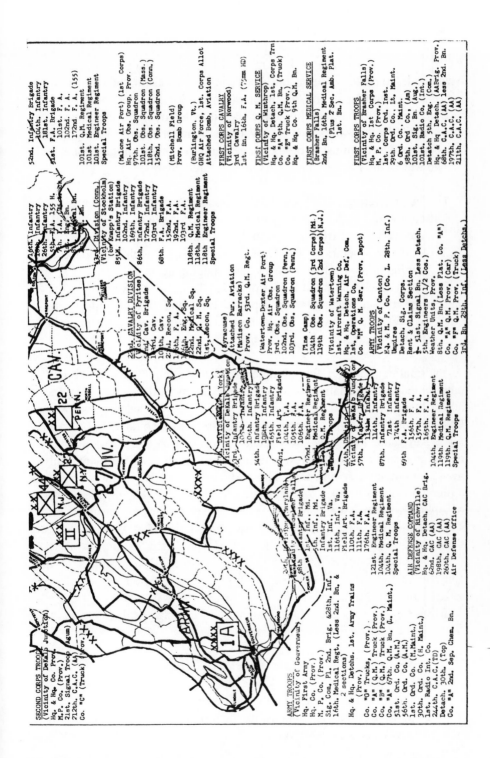

General Marshall knew that the greater danger lay across the Atlantic. Accordingly, it was decided that the United States effort would be concentrated on Germany first with a rear guard action against the Japanese. Meanwhile, to protect Britain and Australia from invasion, the United States continued aid to Britain and the Union of Soviet Socialist Republics (USSR).

Both Roosevelt and Churchill agreed that in order to prevent the almost fatal errors made by the Allies in World War I, national pride must be suppressed and deployed forces must be brought together into a single military command.

The war in the Pacific divided itself into three phases:

1. The long retreat. The United States lost battle after battle and was not able to hold back the enemy anywhere for long in our costly 2,000-mile withdrawal from Luzon to Australia.
2. A holding operation. The United States sparred with the Japanese, lunging at them, drawing back, and lunging again.
3. The long climb up the ladder of little islands all the way from U.S. bases in New Zealand to the Japanese mainland. Initially, this was to be a holding operation, while the United States built up its might in the European theater.

A multinational Allied force, under British command, having fought a determined German/Italian force, advanced yard by yard over adverse terrain, across North Africa, Sicily and up the boot of Italy from Salerno, past Monte Cassino and Anzio, to capture Rome, the first Axis capital to fall to Allied forces, on 5 June 1944. Also by that date, ships of the Allied invasion force, of the long-awaited "second front" designed to crush Nazi Germany, pulled away from their piers in Britain. The next day, General Eisenhower's massive amphibious force hit the Normandy beaches of France. Meanwhile, General MacArthur, having taken advantage of Japanese weaknesses, turned to attack sooner than had been expected. In Italy, Gen. Sir Harold R. L. G. Alexander, Commander of Allied Armies in Italy (AAI), predicted that once Rome had fallen, the Germans probably would withdraw to the Pisa-Rimini or Gothic Line, imposing the maximum delay on our advance by strong mobile rear guards and demolitions.

To execute the expressed Allied intent of destroying hostile forces in Italy, future operations were divided into three phases:

1. Drive the enemy back to the Gothic Line, inflicting maximum losses on him in the process.
2. Penetrate the Gothic Line between Dicomano and Pistoia.
3. Exploit over the Apennines to the Po River Line and establish bridgeheads over that river.

During the two months following the fall of Rome, the Allied Armies in Italy were reduced by nine full infantry divisions and the equivalent of a tenth. The French Expeditionary Corps (FEC) of four divisions and three groups of tabors (goumiers) and the VI (U.S.) Corps of three divisions, two infantry regiments, and three infantry battalion-size units together with a large number of field artillery, engineer, and other supporting units were withdrawn to serve in France. The British 5th Division left for service in the Middle East. This reduction in force left the Allied Armies in Italy (AAI) with the additional mission of holding the maximum German force in Italy and preventing them from being withdrawn for service on their "Western Front." Nevertheless, the Allied Armies in Italy did not tarry after the Germans left Rome but continued to advance rapidly. Pursuit of the Tenth and Fourteenth German Armies and destroying them as much as possible was the order of the day.

Initially, the War Department had envisioned the organization and employment of four black divisions. Three actually came into being. They were the 2nd Cavalry Division, the 93rd Infantry Division, and the 92nd Infantry Division. The 2nd Cavalry Division was sent to North Africa, broken up, and used in port operations. The 93rd Infantry Division was sent to the South Pacific where it was employed in regimental combat team strength in mopping up operations, principally on Bougainville. The 92nd Infantry Division fought in Italy as a division for more than nine months, in extremely rugged terrain, against a determined enemy.

Over 63 percent of the officers within the assigned and attached black elements were black. This encompassed all ranks from 2nd Lieutenant to Colonel. The 597th and 600th FA Battalions, organic to the division, and the 366th Infantry Regiment, attached, were all black. The artillery, technical, and administrative support of the Division was excellent, as was the collection of intelligence and coordination of partisan activities.

Much of the time the 92nd Infantry Division operated with a strength of approximately 25,000 including approximately 10,000 attached troops. The attached troops included a large contingent of British forces. It operated over an exceptionally broad front (at one time, approximately 23 miles). This broad front permitted the concentration of other United States and Allied Forces for launching attacks in other areas.

During the German winter offensive in December 1944, the 92nd Infantry Division was augmented by the 8th Indian Division, regimental combat teams from the 34th and 85th (U.S.) Infantry, the 6th South African Armored Division, and other reinforcements provided by Gen. Mark Clark's 15th Army Group.

When reinforced by the attachment of the 442nd (Japanese-American) and the 473rd (U.S.) Infantry Regiments and other supporting troops, it conducted an offensive operation in the Spring of 1945, with outstanding success, capturing Massa, Carrara, La Spezia, Genoa, and driving to Torino, meeting the French at Bentimiglia and other elements of 15th Army Group in Milan.

When hostilities had ceased in Italy on 2 May 1945, the 92nd Infantry Division, reinforced, had driven from Pontedera, on the Arno River east of Pisa, west and north along the coast of the Ligurian Sea to Genoa, Imperia, Ventimiglia, Cuneo, and Turin, clearing hostile forces from 3,000 square miles and capturing a total of 23,845 prisoners of war.

1.

Rome-Arno Campaign

24 August - 9 September 1944

THE SITUATION

At the time that elements of the 92nd Infantry Division were committed to battle in Italy on 24 August 1944, the Mediterranean Theater of Operation (MTO) was commanded by Field Marshal (then Gen.) Sir Henry Maitland Wilson. As the Supreme Allied Commander, his responsibilities also included North Africa, Greece, Yugoslavia, and Southern France, as well as the sea. Allied forces in Italy included British, South Africans, New Zealanders, Canadians, Poles, Greeks, Italians, Jews, white and black Americans, and Brazilians. The Allied 15th Army Group (known for a time as Headquarters Central Mediterranean Forces and later as Headquarters Allied Armies in Italy) was commanded by Field Marshal (then Gen.) Sir Harold R. L. G. Alexander, and consisted of the U.S. Fifth Army, commanded by Gen. (then Lt. Gen.) Mark W. Clark, and British Eighth Army, commanded by Lt. Gen. Sir Richard L. McCreery.

The Rome-Arno Campaign began on 22 June 1944, following the collapse of the German resistance on the Winter Line, the Gustav Line, the Hitler Line, and the Cordon around the Anzio Beachhead, resulting in the fall of Rome. Field Marshal Albert Kesselring, the Supreme German Commander Southwest and Commander-in-Chief Army Group "C," had at his disposal 25 German divisions and five Fascist Republican Italian divisions. Twenty-one German divisions were assigned to the German Tenth Army commanded by General Vietinghoff and Fourteenth Army commanded by Lt. General Lemelsen. Kesselring directed the Tenth and Fourteenth Armies to pull back towards northern Italy.

After many stubborn rear guard and delaying actions all the way from Rome, many determined stands in terrain that favored the defender, as well as making full use of demolitions and mines, Kesselring called a halt along the Arno River. Behind these positions were the rugged peaks of the North Apennines, reinforced by a series of fixed defenses, known as the Gothic Line.

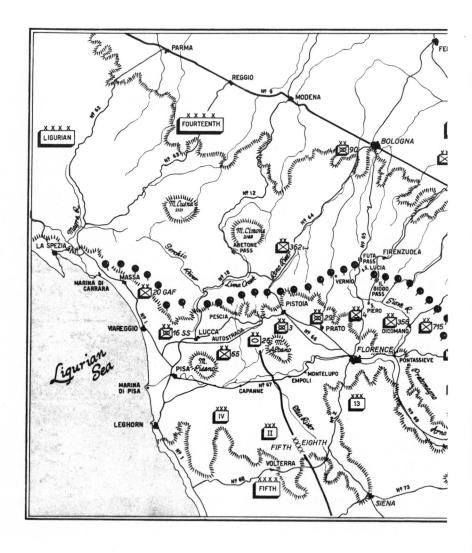

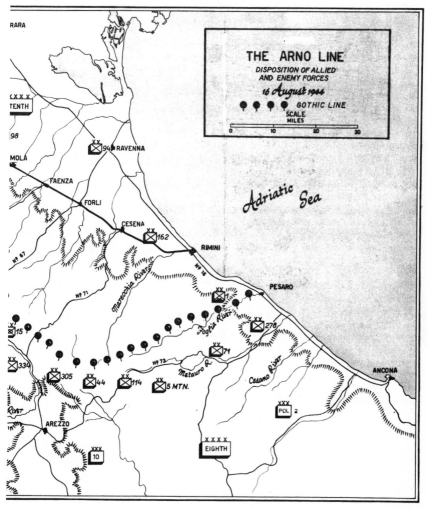

The Germans were determined to hold that line at all cost. Hitler personally directed that any general or general staff officer who prepared withdrawal plans for evacuation of the Gothic Line would be executed.

Six German divisions opposed the U.S. Fifth Army, and 14 opposed the British Eighth Army. One division, the 90th Panzer Grenadier Division under the command of Col. Hans-Joachim Wunderlich,[2] was retained in reserve in the Bologna area. The Fifth and Eighth Armies drove north from Rome and reached the Arno River on 18 July 1944. During the pursuit north of Rome, the Fifth Army was called upon to furnish large forces for the invasion of Southern France. This force included four divisions of the French Expeditionary Corps, and the U.S. VI Corps consisting of the 3rd, 36th, and 45th Infantry Divisions, the 442nd Regimental Combat team, the 517th Parachute Infantry Regiment, the 509th Parachute Infantry Battalion, and the First Special Service Force, as well as artillery engineer and other supporting units assigned to the Seventh Army. The assignment of the 92nd Infantry Division and the Brazilian Division to the Fifth Army fell far short of making up for the loss of two Corps.

After reaching the Arno River, the Fifth Army assumed a defensive attitude. The latter part of July and most of August 1944 was devoted to consolidating forces, resting, restocking, moving supply points forward, and preparing for the assault on the Gothic Line. The deployment of the advanced elements of the 92nd Infantry Division found the troops of the Fifth Army poised along the south bank of the Arno River on a 35-mile front, extending from Marina di Pisa, on the Ligurian coast, to the Elsa River, 20 miles west of Florence. The British Eighth Army had occupied the portion of Florence south of the Arno with the right flank on the Adriatic coast beyond the port of Ancona.

370th REGIMENTAL COMBAT TEAM

Col. Raymond G. Sherman's 370th Regimental Combat Team was assigned to Maj. Gen. Willis D. Crittenberger's IV Corps on 17 August 1944 and to Maj. Gen. Vernon E. Prichard's 1st Armored Division and to Col. Hamilton H. Howze's Combat Command A (CCA) on 18 August 1944. The 1st Armored Division's orders were to hold the enemy on its front and be prepared to resume the offensive on order.

The 370th Infantry Regimental Command Post was established near Ponsaco on 22 August. On the night of 23-24 August, the 3rd Battalion, 370th Infantry, commanded by Lt. Col. Clarence W. Daugette, relieved the 14th Armored Infantry Battalion near Pantedera. On 25 August, the 2nd Battalion, commanded by Lt. Col. George O. Weber, relieved the 6th Armored Infantry south of Pantedera, and on 26 August the 1st Battalion, commanded by Lt. Col. Ernest V. Murphy, Jr., occupied reserve positions on the extreme right of the Regimental sector. On 23 August, the 598th Field Artillery Battalion, under the command of Lt. Col. Robert C. Ross, took up position in support of the Regiment.

At dawn on 24 August, C Battery, 598th Field Artillery Battalion, fired on the enemy for the first time. Subsequently, hostile counter-battery fire resulted in a tree burst, and 1st Sgt. Jerry B. Davis of A Battery was seriously wounded.

A small salient south of the Arno River, in the 2nd Battalion area, was held by the Germans. This was a threat to the security of the entire line. The area was well covered with anti-personnel mines. On 29 August, the 370th Infantry was ordered to drive the enemy from this area, and to push the line forward to the Arno. G Company seized the objective within an hour, and with the aid of E Company and additional artillery fire it beat off two counterattacks. By 0700 on 30 August, the disputed area was firmly in the hands of the 2nd Battalion.

These 105 mm guns of the 598th Field Artillery Battalion are delivering the first artillery fire of the 92nd Division on hostile positions in Italy, 24 August 1944.

On 30 August, Lt. Jake Chandler, accompanied by Capt. Charles F. Gandy, led a 22-man patrol from F Company across the Arno. The patrol destroyed an enemy machine gun position and captured two German soldiers. Both prisoners tried to escape, but enemy fire killed one and wounded the other. This was the first patrol that Fifth Army had put across the Arno. It was determined that although the area was heavily fortified with mines, automatic weapons, and heavy armor, enemy strength was relatively light. As a consequence, General Clark directed the Fifth Army to resume the offensive.

The 370th Infantry was ordered with other CCA and IV Corps units to cross the Arno at 1000 on 1 September. The Regimental Objective was the capture of Mount Pisano, a walnut-shaped mountain about three miles wide and six miles long. All three battalions of the 370th Infantry (except C Company, which was then attached to Combat Command B [CCB]) crossed the river on the morning of 1 September with the 1st and 2nd Battalions on the east and the 3rd Battalion on the west. Direct artillery support was provided by the 598th Field Artillery Battalion to the 1st and 2nd Battalions and by the 91st Armored Field Artillery Battalion to the 3rd Battalion. Mines and sniper fire were the chief sources of resistance. By dark, the attacking troops had advanced two to three miles north of the river. During the night the 598th and 91st Field Artillery Battalions forded the river and occupied positions north of it. B Company, 317th Engineer (C) Battalion, cleared the mines and improved fords, and by 0300 on 2 September had a class-30 treadway bridge in operation near Pontedera. On 2 September, the 3rd Battalion skirted the west side of Mount Pisano and reached the banks of the Serchio River west of the walled city of Lucca. The 1st Battalion, with one company riding on tanks of the 1st Tank Battalion, 1st Armored Division, moved forward for six miles around the east side of the mountain to positions on the northeast slope. The 2nd Battalion followed mule trails directly into the hill mass. Mount Pisano was taken by the end of 2 September, and the 370th Infantry command post was moved to Uliveto.

For the next three days the German 65th Grenadier Division continued to withdraw to the Gothic Line covering its movements with rear guard action and artillery fire. The 370th Infantry continued its advance towards the ancient walled city of Lucca. At about 1000 on 3 September, an Italian partisan reported that the partisans had driven the Germans from the city and closed the gate. He stated that the city was without food, and its water supply had been shut off when the retreating Germans destroyed the viaduct. He requested that American troops enter the city and take control as soon as possible.

Maj. A. R. Biggs, Regimental Executive Officer, was killed on 4 September by artillery fire in the vicinity of Ripafratta. A platoon of F Company, with tank support, patrolled Lucca and reconnoitered the west and south gates. The

Using seized local rowboats, men of the 370th Infantry Regiment crossed the Arno River, 1 September 1944.

2nd Battalion, although receiving heavy small artillery fire, moved forward and by dark reached the Canale Reggio. Early on the morning of 5 September, E Company entered Lucca, and F Company moved in in the afternoon. The city was quiet except for occasional automatic weapons fire.

The 3rd Battalion, facing small arms, machine gun, and artillery fire, cleared the Autostrada from Pisa to Lucca. The 1st Battalion advanced about 2½ miles east of Lucca. The Regimental Command Post was moved forward and established in a hotel in Lucca. The 598th Field Artillery Battalion moved forward to the vicinity of Lucca and established a battalion OP in the top of the Cathedral bell tower. The Anti-Tank Company, 370th Infantry, established a mobile perimeter defense around the city.

Once Lucca was taken, General Clark directed that the IV Corps regroup its forces, consolidate its positions, maintain contact with the enemy, be prepared to move forward in the event the enemy continued to withdraw north, and form a task force of armor and infantry for possible employment under II Corps control. The rapid advance by the IV Corps had not been anticipated. A temporary halt was called in order for II Corps, the Army's main effort, to initiate its offensive. The 370th Infantry brought up its right flank to positions paralleling the Serchio River.

In defense of their position, the Germans employed at least one and possibly two huge railroad guns, either 28 cm or 38 cm caliber. The guns were hidden in railroad tunnels just north of Lucca and brought into the open to fire, then immediately retreated to the safety of the tunnels. American personnel referred to them as "one round" guns because only one round was necessary to destroy a huge building. The Germans intended for these guns to attack the morale of U.S. forces. They were aimed primarily at Lucca and its outskirts; thus their fire had little or no effect on American personnel. At that time, the 370th Regimental Combat Team had, for the most part, cleared the built-up area of the city.

A 598th Field Artillery Battalion forward observer reported that a U.S. jeep had been hit by hostile machine gun fire and abandoned upside down in a deep ravine about 500 yards in front of our leading elements. He also reported that he thought the enemy had pulled back from that area. Major Arnold, the Battalion Executive Officer, with a few men from Service Battery, 598th Field Artillery Battalion, and a 3/4-ton vehicle, inched forward into the area and recovered the jeep. This vehicle was repaired, painted, and designated HQ26-598FA (Headquarters Battery, 598th Field Artillery Battalion was authorized 25 vehicles) and became Arnold's personal vehicle for the duration including his service with the 88th Division on the Morgan Line. By the end of the war, he had also made good use of two Fiats and one Opel. After capture, they were painted olive drab and marked with U.S. insignias.

On the way back from recovering this vehicle, Major Arnold stopped by

Troops of the 92nd Division in action along a canal north of Lucca.

Regimental Headquarters to advise Colonel Sherman of the situation on his front. At that time, Colonel Sherman was in conference with representatives of the 1st Armored Division, so Major Arnold asked the Regimental Operations Sergeant, Sergeant Parks (formerly an undertaker from Washington, D.C.), "Why don't your troops move forward? There are no enemy within 500 yards of your front." Sergeant Parks' response was, "ain't no villers there and we have become house broke." (Translation: Stone houses in northern Italy make good fortified positions. Since there are none there, we will not move through that open area until we resume the attack.)

After 6 September, General Clark ordered that aggressive reconnaissance patrols be pushed well forward to maintain contact and to create the impression that an attack was forming on the 1st Armored Division front. This resulted in minor gains by the 370th Infantry, as well as other elements, along the division front.

2.

North Apennines
Campaign

10 September 1944 - 4 April 1945

Snow-capped peaks of the Apennines in the Serchio Valley sector give an idea of the rugged country with stone villages and narrow fields.

THE TERRAIN

The mountain barrier facing Fifth Army, known as the Northern Apennines, extends from the Ligurian Alps, south of Genoa, southeast across the Italian peninsula, nearly to the Adriatic Sea, below Rimini. On the north side, the Northern Apennines meet the broad fertile plain of the Po River in a slightly curved, clear-cut line. To the south, on the Fifth Army side, they drop away to the narrow coastal plain along the Ligurian Sea in an irregular line to various plains along the Arno River. At its narrowest point, between Florence and Bologna, the range is approximately 50 miles wide. Individual mountains rise to heights up to 7,095 feet, making the Northern Apennines at all points a deep and formidable obstacle to an advance into the Po Valley.

The ill-defined summit line lies close to the southern edge of the range, so that the slopes facing south are generally steep while those facing north are relatively long and moderate. The mountains rise from an elevation of 300 feet at the Po Valley to an average crest of 3,000 to 4,000 feet.

The principal river valleys carry roads which cross the mountains by low passes over the watersheds. Generally, the roads run northeast-southwest. A single exception is the Florence-Bologna road, which follows a north-south axis. Highway 1 runs along the flat coastal plain on the Ligurian Sea from Pisa to La Spezia and on through the mountains to Genoa. Seven state roads connect the Arno and Po Valleys. From La Spezia, on the west coast, Highway 62 goes to Parma and Highway 63 to Reggio. Highway 12, in the Serchio River Valley, connects Lucca and Modena. Highway 64 runs from Pistoia to Bologna. Three roads cross the mountains from Florence: Highway 65 to Bologna, Highway 67 to Forli, and Highway 71 to Cesena. The passes of these roads over ridges vary in elevation from 296 feet to 4,553 feet.

Late in September, the fall rains begin. Mountain streams, virtually dry in the summer months, change to raging torrents in a few hours' time, and fog and mist often reduce visibility to near zero. By late October, snow begins to

An old straight Roman road, Highway 1 marked the boundary between the coastal plain and the center of the Division sector. Porta, in the center of the photograph, was an enemy strong point, tying in their defense on the flat ground with that in the mountains.

The remains of the medieval fortress above the D-file at Porta on Highway 1. Such old fortified positions were used by both sides both as observation posts and as infantry strong points and were hard to demolish with normal field artillery.

fall on the higher peaks, and in mid-winter the mountain passes are sometimes blocked to traffic for short periods.

The German name for their fortification of this mountain range was Goten Stellung or Gothic Line. Construction of these defenses began shortly after Italy's capitulation in September 1943. The Gothic Line extended approximately 170 miles across the Italian peninsula from Pesaro on the Adriatic coast to the mountains north of Pisa on the west coast. It was constructed by the German Todt Organization, employing German engineers and a large number of impressed Italian laborers. It was sited to take maximum advantage of the rugged mountains and the limited number of access roads. In general, it followed the southern side of the water divide, rather than the crestline.

At some points, the line was several miles deep. The scarcity of traversable roads made continuous defenses unnecessary and allowed the concentration of the strongest obstacles at key positions. These strong points were spiked with mine fields, tank traps, concrete-embedded artillery, machine gun emplacements, anti-tank and anti-aircraft guns, and strongly fortified stations for riflemen. Automatic weapons were mutually supporting. Interlocking fields of fire covered wide areas of terrain. Many of the fortifications were carved into the mountains, whereas in some sectors, tank turrets were placed in concrete.

The Germans intended to hold the Gothic Line to prevent the Allies from occupying the Po Valley and the industrial and agricultural northland of Italy. They apparently intended to incorporate this region as a buffer to the redoubt, built around Berchtesgaden, Germany, that Hitler announced would be able to hold out for 1,000 years. The Gothic Line was to be held at all cost.

PIERCING THE GOTHIC LINE

General Clark's plan of attack on the Gothic Line envisioned the Army's main effort being made by the II Corps on the eight-mile front, beginning five miles east of Florence and extending to Pontassieve. To permit the concentration of II Corps troops for the attack north of Florence, the 6th South African Armored Division was detached from the British 13 Corps and attached to the U.S. IV Corps.

When General Clark, on 9 September, issued orders for the Fifth Army attack, all restrictions on the advance of the IV Corps were lifted. On the morning of 10 September, the entire Fifth Army front erupted in an offensive against the main defenses of the Gothic Line. The 2nd Battalion, 370th Infantry, crossed the Serchio River on a front extending from Lucca west to Ponte San Pietro and began clearing the hills on the west side of the river while the 1st Battalion pushed north over the last few miles of plain on the east side of the river. The 3rd Battalion was placed in reserve south of Lucca. The 598th Field Artillery Battalion, with the Cannon Company, 370th Infantry (referred to as D Battery, 598th Field Artillery Battalion) attached, moved to positions north of Lucca in order to stay within supporting range.

The value of partisan aid now became apparent. In addition to supplying information about the location of enemy positions, they performed destructive missions on their own and in cooperation with the attacking troops. On 13 September, when A Company, 370th Infantry, riding on and supported by tanks, fought its way into Ponte a Moriana, four miles upstream from Lucca, the regiment had reached the foothills of the Northern Apennines.

As the 42nd Jaeger Division withdrew, major obstacles were created by the destruction of bridges, blown roads on the side of mountains, and other roadblocks. The advance was marked by frequent sharp encounters with small groups of the enemy. Hostile artillery fire was increased. The 598th Field Artillery Battalion began its own program of harassing fire. The 1st Armored

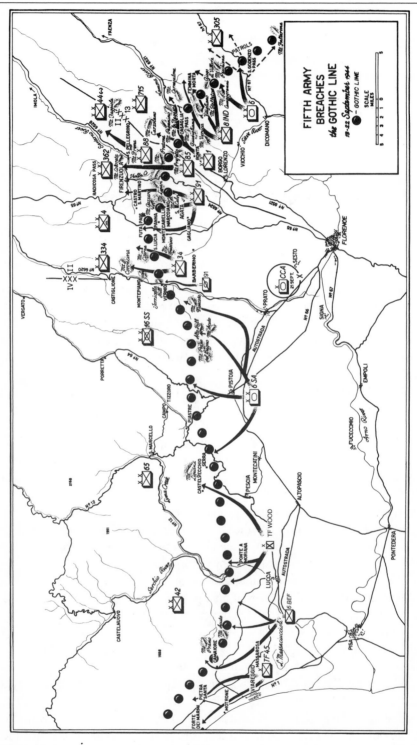

Division was operating on a 20-mile front with two of its infantry battalions completely out of action. Armor could be used only to a limited extent in the mountains, and the 81st Cavalry Reconnaissance Squadron was forced to become in effect a mountain infantry unit.

On 13 September, the 3rd Battalion, 370th Infantry, was pulled out of reserve and moved up the west bank of the Serchio River, through the 2nd Battalion, to a line located on the Nobilli-Aquitea-Via Praducci line. On this same day, orders were received from Fifth Army that the 1st Armored Division was to be employed in such a way as to permit the movement of the division, less one combat command, on 48-hours' notice to an assembly area near Florence.

On 16 September, IV Corps ordered a renewed effort to prevent the enemy from withdrawing troops from the front. An attack all along the 370th Infantry front was launched on 17 September, screened by artillery smoke projectiles. The 2nd and 3rd Battalions, on the west side of the Serchio, attacked northward through the hills with substantial gains. The Regimental Command Post was moved to Moriana on the morning of 17 September. Combat Command A, 1st Armored Division, was removed on 18 September and for the first time the 370th Regimental Combat Team was on its own.

The Germans resisted with artillery, machine gun, mortar, and Nebelwerfer fire. Seventeen rockets fell on the 3rd Battalion south of Mount Castellaccio. In spite of enemy resistance, the 370th Infantry continued to move up the Serchio Valley, mopping up strong points in its zone. Bitter fighting developed on the west of the Serchio on Mount Castellaccio, over 1,800 feet high. Hostile forces were determined to hold this position. After three days of skillful use of fire and maneuver, the 3rd Battalion overcame hostile resistance. After the capture of Mount Castellaccio, it became obvious why the hostile forces had fought so tenaciously. The backside of the mountain was a sheer cliff. The defending forces had been supplied by cable that was capable of handling only ammunition and rations.

The 370th Infantry continued its attack on 19 September. After a number of close-range fire fights, it advanced to the vicinity of Ponte Madailena and Bagni di Lucca. On 21 September, the 1st Battalion, 370th Infantry, relieved the 14th Armored Infantry Battalion on the right, and on 24 September, the 2nd Battalion, 370th Infantry, was shifted to replace the 6th Armored Infantry Battalion. The 1st Armored Division, less Combat Command B (CCB), was transferred from the IV Corps to the II Corps.

Command of 370th Regimental Combat Team and CCB together with responsibility for the zone of the 1st Armored Division was passed to Task Force Wood, commanded by Brig. General Wood, Assistant Division Commander of the 92nd Division. His staff was made up of a small advance group from the 92nd Division Headquarters. The 6th Regimental Combat Team, 1st

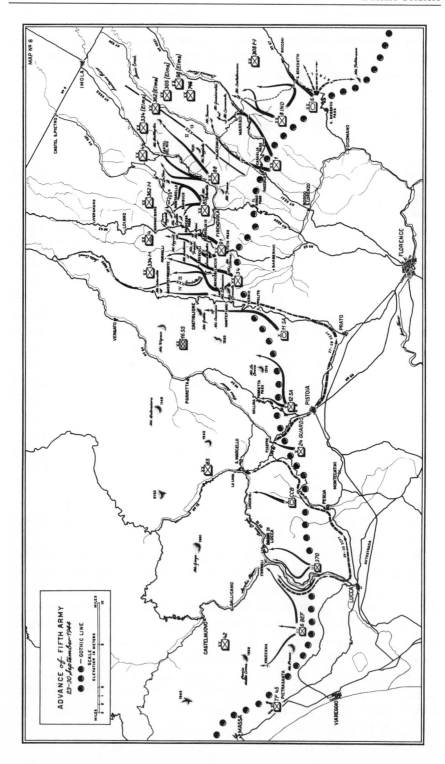

Brazilian Division, moved between the 370th Infantry Regiment's left flank and Task Force 45, relieving the 3rd Battalion on the east of the Serchio River. The 3rd Battalion relieved elements of CCB in the vicinity of S. Marcello and, on 29 September, pushed north to La Lima. The 1st and 2nd Battalions continued through the mountains, north of Mount Prano, west of the Serchio, to the vicinity of Bagni di Lucca. The 2nd Battalion was on the right and the 1st Battalion on the left. Task Force Wood was reduced to the 370th Infantry with a zone 20 miles wide. The 370th Regimental Command Post moved to Prunetta.

The 598th Field Artillery Battalion was divided into two. A and B Batteries under Major Arnold, Battalion Executive Officer, occupied positions in the vicinity of La Lima in support of the 1st Battalion, and C Battery and Cannon Company, under Major Starbuck, Battalion S-3, remained in the Serchio in support of the 2nd and 3rd Battalions. Lt. Col. Robert C. Ross, Commanding Officer, 598th Field Artillery Battalion, joined the staff of Task Force Wood.

On 1 October, the 3rd Battalion continued its advance up Highway 12 with its flank to Cutiglina.[3] The Regimental Command Post moved to San Marcello. On 2 October, the 2nd Battalion moved, under the cover of darkness, to positions southeast of Viareggio, on the Ligurian coast. On 3 October, the 1st Battalion moved to the coast. Night movements were made with lights behind the light line; *i.e.*, just beyond artillery range. There was no enemy air action. On 3 October, the 2nd Battalion relieved the 39th Light Anti-Artillery Battalion (dismounted and fighting as infantry) just north of Pietrasanta. The 1st Battalion moved to an assembly area in the vicinity of Viareggio. The 598th Field Artillery Battalion moved to positions in the vicinity of Pietrasanta and was attached to Task Force 45 as was the 179th Chemical Smoke Generating Company.

On 5 October, the 370th Regiment established its command post in the vicinity of Pietrasanta and assumed control of its 2nd Battalion. On 5 October, Task Force Wood became Task Force 92 under the command of Maj. Gen. Edward M. Almond, Commanding General, 92nd Infantry Division, with responsibility for the coastal sector extending from Forte dei Marmi on the coast to the left boundary of the 1st Brazilian Division.

The 370th Regimental Combat Team had been in the line 42 days. It had sustained 263 casualties: 19 killed, 225 wounded, and 19 missing. It had advanced almost 30 miles against resistance that included small arms, machine guns, and automatic weapons in fixed positions and heavy artillery fire. It had penetrated the Gothic Line and cleared the east-west portion of Highway 12 in front of the IV Corps.

Task Force 92 was formed in the badly damaged resort of Viareggio.

TASK FORCE 92

Task Force 92, replacing Task Force Wood, was formed in the vicinity of Viareggio, Italy, on 5 October 1944, under the command of Maj. Gen. Edward M. Almond, Commanding General, 92nd Infantry Division. It included the 370th Regimental Combat Team, including the 598th Field Artillery Battalion, the 2nd Armored Group with the 434th and 435th Anti-Aircraft Artillery Battalions, dismounted and fought as infantry, the 751st Tank Battalion, the 894th Tank Destroyer Battalion, 179th Chemical (SG) Company, C Battery 351st Anti-Aircraft Artillery (SL) Battalion, C Battery 450th Anti-Aircraft Artillery (AW) Battalion, and 2nd Company 23rd Engineer Battalion (Italian).

Col. Frank E. Barber, Chief of Staff, 92nd Division, was killed on 3 October, his third day in Italy. Lt. Col. William J. McCaffrey became Chief of Staff.

Late in the afternoon of 5 October, Maj. Thomas St. John Arnold, Executive Officer, 598th Field Artillery Battalion, was directed to report to the Command Post by 1700 to assume the duties of Assistant Chief of Staff G-3, 92nd Infantry Division. Other members of the General Staff were Maj. Charles F. Mock, Jr., Assistant Chief of Staff, G-1; Lt. Col. Donald M. MacWillie, Assistant Chief of Staff, G-2; and Lt. Col. John T. Lorenz, Assistant Chief of Staff, G-4.

The next day, Task Force 92 launched its first concerted action to capture Mount Cauala as an initial objective for the capture of Massa. When Major Arnold reported for duty on the Division staff, General Almond said to him, "I want this Division to go farther, fire more ammunition, capture more terrain, and kill or capture more of the enemy than it would if anyone else was its commander. As my G-3, it is your job to assist me in seeing that this is accomplished." The offensive along the coast got under way at 0600 on 6 October, following a two-hour artillery preparation, with the 1st and 2nd Battalions, 370th Infantry, attacking abreast against Mount Cauala and the

Huge railroad and coastal defense guns were abandoned in the vicinity of Viareggio. A derailed railroad heavy gun and its carriage lie to the left with two heavy coastal weapons on permanent mountings in the center.

434th and 435th Anti-Aircraft Artillery Battalions bringing up the left flank between Highway 1 and the sea. An advance of slightly over one mile was made on the right and slight gains were made near the coast, but heavy rains and insufficient reconnaissance hampered the troops. Tanks and tank destroyers attached to the 2nd Armored Group were ordered to support the attack along Highway 1 on the morning of 7 October. They were blocked by lack of suitable stream crossings over the swollen creeks, and no progress was made. The next day the 2nd Battalion, 370th Infantry, was driven back by mortar and artillery fire when it reached the upper slopes of Mount Cauala. The battalion regrouped after dark. At 0300 on 9 October, the troops moved forward again, scaled the steep rocks below the summit, and reached the crest without opposition. In the afternoon, mortar and artillery fire forced a second withdrawal. On the left the 435th Anti-Aircraft Artillery Battalion, aided by two platoons of Sherman tanks of the 751st Tank Battalion, seized the cemetery just north of Querceta.

Meanwhile, the I & R Platoon, 370th Infantry, reached Seravezza, where it was to establish contact with elements of the 1st Brazilian Division. Despite very heavy small-arms fire from the heights of Mount Cauala, the troops cleared Seravezza of enemy snipers, but were unable to contact the Brazilians. On the extreme left, the Reconnaissance Company, 894th Tank Destroyer Battalion, patrolled the Ligurian coast and maintained the security of the Task Force left flank from the Arno River north to Forte dei Marmi.

For the next two days, Task Force 92 made preparations to resume the attack on Mount Cauala. Ladders were constructed for the assault against the cliffs, and crossings were sought over Seravezza Creek, which was badly swollen by the steady rains. On the evening of 11 October, the 2nd and 3rd Battalions, 370th Infantry, crossed the creek and started up the mountain. Their companies reached the summit at 0730 the next morning; by late afternoon artillery and mortar fire again made their positions untenable. No further effort was made to take the mountain until the night of 17-18 October when a patrol fought its way to the crest of Mount Strettoia. On 19 October, the patrol was relieved by a platoon, and the positions were further reinforced the next day. The road through Seravezza was opened for jeeps. After efforts to expand the hold on Mount Cauala by taking the next height to the northeast failed on 23 October, the offensive along the coast was halted.

The disposition of enemy units also was changed. The 42nd Jaeger Division extended its lines to include the Serchio Valley, but an additional unit was required to defend the central area. This gap was filled by the 232nd Grenadier Regiment, a new unit made up of personnel on leave from the Russian front and men from 35 to 45 years of age. Late in the month, the 42nd Light Division was withdrawn with the exception of a few troops left in the Serchio Valley to bolster elements of the Monte Rosa Alpine Division, the first of the

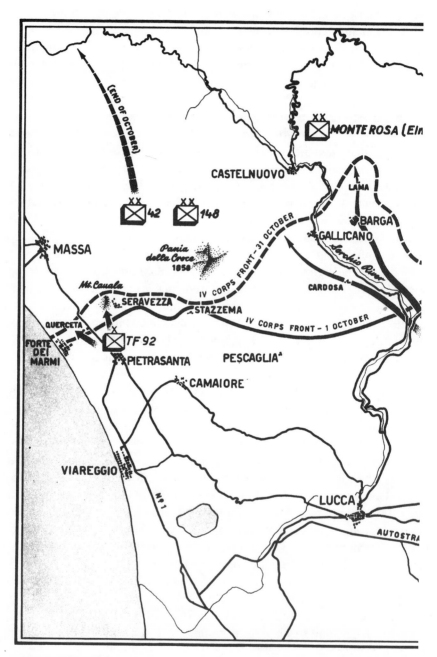

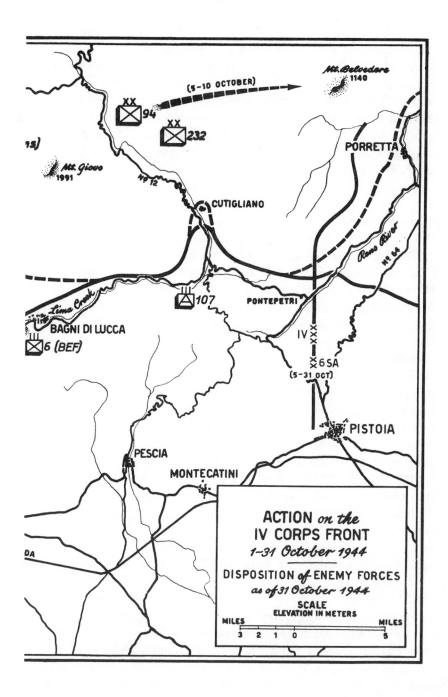

ACTION *on the*
IV CORPS FRONT
1–31 October 1944

DISPOSITION *of* ENEMY FORCES
as of 31 October 1944

SCALE
ELEVATION IN METERS

reorganized Italian Republican (Fascist) Divisions to be used against the Allies, and elements of the Italian San Marco Division. This former reserve unit, after being driven across the French-Italian frontier by Seventh Army, was converted into a field division in the Genoa area.

Meanwhile, a system of vigorous reinforced patrols was undertaken, to keep the enemy off balance, discover weak spots, and exploit the element of maneuver. These "power patrols" sent out on probing missions were miniature assault teams. They consisted of reinforced platoons with light machine gun teams, 60-mm mortar squads, artillery forward observers, litter bearers, signal flares, and radio equipment. These patrols pecked away at Mount Cauala and resulted in slight gains on the coast. Plans were being prepared for an advance on the coast that involved crossing of the Cinquale Canal at its mouth. This stream was about 100 feet wide and 20 feet deep. In order to facilitate a possible crossing, the 317th Engineer (C) Battalion, commanded by Lt. Col. Edward L. Rowney, constructed a dam across its source in the foothills of the North Apennines. Over a period of time, this caused much of the low area to be inundated. The dam was subsequently removed.

During the later part of October, the main body of the 92nd Division arrived in Italy and staged at Leghorn. Each new arrival prepared to enter the line on call. Beginning on 31 October, elements of Col. James Notestein's 371st Infantry Regiment, which had arrived at Leghorn ón 18 October, moved to replace the 370th Infantry. Lt. Col. Theodore A. Kimpton's 1st Battalion was committed on 31 October, and Maj. John J. Hazel's 3rd Battalion was committed on 2 November. The relief of the 3rd Battalion, 370th Infantry, by the 1st Battalion, 371st Infantry, was made under the cover of darkness. Just before the relief was completed, it was reported to Assistant Chief of Staff G-3 that they were on the line with no ammunition. (To prevent accidents, troops in training were not issued ammunition.) The situation was quickly corrected when the Assistant Chief of Staff G-2 directed that the 3rd Battalion, 370th Infantry, turn over one-half of its basic lead of ammunition to the 1st Battalion, 371st Infantry. Maj. George E. Pinard's 2nd Battalion moved into position as regimental reserve on 12 November. The 370th Infantry was shifted to the east to replace the 1st Brazilian Division in the Serchio Valley. This relief occurred over a three-day period. General Almond's Task Force 92 was now responsible for a 23-mile sector.

On 4 November, Task Force 92 was deployed with the 2nd Armored Group on the left flank, holding the coastal plain; the 371st Infantry was deployed in the center with its regimental command post at Pietrasanta; and the 370th Infantry, with the 598th Field Artillery Battalion in support, was deployed on the right in the Serchio Valley near Gallicano and Barga. On moving to the Serchio Valley, the 370th Infantry was directed to establish contact with the 1st Brazilian Division. The Regiment dispatched a platoon for this purpose. Later, when it was reported that the platoon was in a fire fight well to the rear of the leading elements, it was realized that the fire fight was with a platoon of the 1st Brazilian Division dispatched for the same purpose. Fortunately, no one was hurt. The next day Major Arnold, the Assistant Chief of Staff G-3, visited the Assistant Chief of Staff G-3, IV Corps, to arrange for better contact between the 92nd Division and the 1st Brazilian Division. While Major Arnold was at the IV Corps command post, the IV Corps Assistant Chief of Staff G-3 received a report from the 1st Brazilian Division regarding an attack by a German power patrol. However, the only information the IV Corps Assistant Chief of Staff G-3 was able to receive in English was "But sir, two officers were killed." C Battery 450th AAA (AW) Battalion, and C Battery 351st AAA (SL) Battalion, had been detached. Casualties during this period were 32 killed, 223 wounded, and 110 missing in action for a total of 365. A total of 124 prisoners of war had been captured.

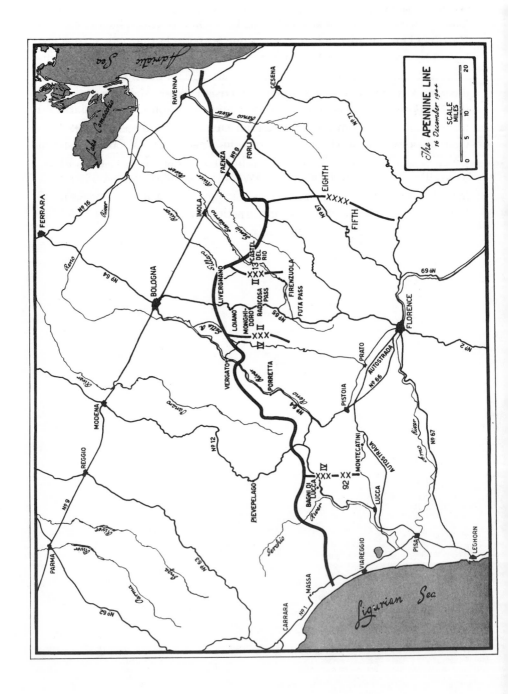

92nd Division on the Offensive

By the end of October, the enemy had massed its strength to cover Bologna against the attack of Fifth Army. As a result of this and the torrential rains, mud-clogged supply routes, and snow in the high elevations, the Fifth Army's drive towards Bologna gradually slowed to a halt. On 2 November, the Army assumed an attitude of active defense while regrouping and preparing for resumption of the offensive in December.

While Task Force 92 was probing with power patrols in the Serchio Valley and on the coast, the main body of the 92nd Division was arriving in Italy and staging at Leghorn. On 4 November, the 92nd Division came under the direct control of Fifth Army, with responsibility for a 23-mile wide coastal sector. Its mission was to hold maximum enemy forces in the coastal area, exert pressure, and protect Fifth Army's left flank. Thus, the Division's coverage of this unusually broad front permitted the concentration of other elements of Fifth Army for the resumption of the offensive. The Division Command Post was established at Viareggio with an advanced command post, under Brig. General Wood, in the Serchio Valley. Task Force 92 no longer existed. The Division Forward Command Post was established under canvas and in vans next to the Principe de Piemonte Hotel with most of the officers billeted in the hotel.

The Commanding General's Mess, for General Almond and his personnel and General Staff, was established in a casino across the street. The foyer of the casino contained a round fountain about 12 feet in diameter. A circular table was constructed around the fountain for the Commanding General and his principal staff. The 92nd Division Band played soft dinner music each evening. After General Almond left the building the band would break into loud jazz and/or boogie-woogie. An officers club, with a bar operated by an Italian named Luegi, was established in the Principe de Piemonte Hotel. Subsequently, as a result of much loose talk by officers at the bar, the Assistant

Principe de Piemonte, Officers Quarters, 92nd Division, Forward Command Post. The hotel, named for the Italian political subdivision, the Principality of Piedmont, was requisitioned as were many large solid buildings during the campaign.

Chiefs of Staff G-2 and G-3 suspected Luegi of being an enemy agent and put him in jail for a month. Since these suspicions could not be confirmed, he was returned to the bar and much later, when the Division Command Post was moved to Genoa, he was taken there to operate the bar at the Golden Spider. After the war Luegi acquired possession of the Principe de Piemonte Hotel. The source of his funds was never determined.

The Division Rear Command Post was established in another hotel, a few blocks away, in Viareggio. An officers club, with a bar, was established in the Division Rear Hotel. Monthly dues were charged for membership in the Division Forward Club. No dues were charged for membership in the Division Rear Club. At a later date, a 92nd Division Stockade was established at a prominent crossroad, within hostile artillery range, south of Pietrasanta. The stockade consisted of a barbed wire enclosure with no buildings. Machine guns were posted at corners with killing zones down each side. Those confined were permitted to take with them their field equipment, including shelter hat and blanket. Because the crossroad was frequently the target of hostile artillery harassing and interdiction fire, the inmates were required to live in foxholes. They were issued dry rations which they could heat over open fire (which could also draw hostile artillery fire) if they so desired. Of course, this was unpleasant duty for the Military Police guarding the stockade. It was necessary to relieve them frequently.

The 424th Field Artillery Group, subsequently commanded by Col. Wellington A. (Sammy) Samouce, functioned as the Division Artillery. Lt. Col. Marcus H. Ray's 600th (Medium) Field Artillery Battalion occupied its initial positions on 2 November. A Detachment of the 5th Battery, 8th Survey Regiment (British), to provide the requisite target acquisition for counterbattery fire was attached on 4 November. The British 71st (less 229th Battery) and 76th Heavy Anti-Aircraft Regiments were also attached on 4 November and employed in a surface role. They provided counter-battery and harassing fire. Lt. Col. Forrest E. Love's 84th Chemical Mortar Battalion and the British 71st Heavy Anti-Aircraft Regiment were employed to provide artillery support in the Serchio Valley. Other British units attached at that time included the 62nd Anti-Aircraft Brigade, the 56th Light Anti-Aircraft Regiment (less 168th Battery), 47th Light Anti-Aircraft Regiment, and the 53rd Anti-Aircraft Operations Room.

Brig. Gen. William H. Colbern's 92nd Division Artillery Headquarters was moved into position in Forte dei Marmi on 8 November and relieved the 424th Field Artillery Group of operational control of the Division Artillery on 10 November. Lt. Col. Edward L. Rowney's 317th Engineer (Combat) Battalion occupied positions in support of the Division on 8 November. The Italian 2nd Company, 23rd Engineer Battalion, was assigned for operational control. Shortly after the arrival of the 317th Engineer Battalion, they were directed to

Commanding General's Mess, Viareggio, Italy.

build a bridge over the deep 20-foot gorge running through Seravezza. The job was given to the Battalion Executive Officer and one platoon. General Almond became frustrated over the delay in construction caused by intermittent hostile machine gun fire. After watching the engineer take cover from time to time, he said, "My aide can do a better job. Take your Engineers away. Aide, build the bridge." Everyone left the area except the aide. It took him all night and much Italian help. However, by dawn the aide had a jeep bridge in place made from telephone poles and lumber from near-by buildings.

The life of General Almond's aides-de-camp was not an easy one. They were expected to be abreast of the situation at all times. On one occasion, when General Almond, accompanied by the Assistant Chief of Staff G-3 and one of his aides, was returning from visiting General Clark, commanding the Fifth Army in Florence, the aide was severely reprimanded for not familiarizing himself with the history of Florence.

Col. John D. Armstrong's 365th Infantry arrived in Italy on 29 October. On 8 November its 2nd Battalion, commanded by Lt. Col. Howard C. Schwarz,

On occasions, the pigeoneer complained that his pigeons were being overworked carrying messages from patrols deep in hostile territory and reports of contact by flank units in the high rugged mountains. Two pigeon lofts of the 209th Signal Pigeon Company were located in the Serchio Valley and two on the coastal plain.

relieved the 435th Anti-Aircraft Battalion from its infantry roll. Maj. Jesse E. Johnston's 1st Battalion entered the line on 13 November, and Lt. Col. Lawrence R. Lashley's 3rd Battalion moved into position as regimental reserve.

The 92nd Cavalry Reconnaissance Troop was committed on 13 November with the mission of protecting the Division right flank and maintaining contact with friendly forces there. Later, the mission of the Troop was changed to the occupation of the central portion of the Division front, a sector approximately 8,000 yards in width, in extremely rugged mountainous terrain. To facilitate the transmission of messages from patrols in mountainous terrain, as well as those deep behind enemy lines, four pigeon lofts of the 209th Signal Pigeon Company was attached to the Division. Two lofts were deployed in the Serchio Valley and two lofts were stationed with the Division Headquarters in the coastal sector. Report of contact between elements in the coastal sector and those in the Serchio Valley by pigeon frequently arrived at Division Headquarters as much as four hours ahead of that by surface means.

Deep patrols behind enemy lines usually carried five pigeons in a small cage. On one occasion, the fifth pigeon brought the message "send more pigeons." In response, a cage with five pigeons was dropped by parachute by a light aircraft of the Division Aviation section over a designated location. Some time passed before any message from the patrol was received. Finally, a lone pigeon returned with a message in German: "The chicken was good. Please send more." The pigeons were utilized to such an extent that the Chief Pigeoneer complained to the Assistant Chief of Staff G-3 that his pigeons were being overworked and badly needed a rest.

To facilitate operations in the mountains, a four-company, 92nd Division Pack Battalion (Provisional) was organized under the command of Lt. Hugh Hanley. For this purpose, Italian mules were requisitioned, and local Italians were used as Mule Skinners. Both Italian men and women were used as porters to transport rations and ammunition in the mountainous areas.

The 34th Quartermaster War Dog Platoon, which was attached on 4 November, was employed to guard the Division Command Post, rations, and other vital supply dumps through the hours of darkness. By the morning of 14 November, the entire 92nd Division was deployed against the enemy, with the exception of Lt. Col. Wendell T. Derricks' 597th Field Artillery Battalion which occupied its initial positions on 15 November. The 434th and 435th Anti-Aircraft Battalions were detached, placed under Fifth Army control, moved to an Army training area, and reorganized and trained as the 473rd Infantry Regiment.

It became evident, shortly after the Division was committed to combat, that the organization and use of Italian partisans would be a considerable assistance in intelligence and operations. A number of British #1 Special Force officers and other ranks had been dropped deep behind enemy lines to organize partisan organizations. Under the direction of the Assistant Chief of Staff G-2, Lt. Col. Donald M. MacWillie, a system was devised to use partisans from the front lines to a depth of 20 miles behind the enemy.

Major Oldham of the British Indian Forces, a #1 Special Force officer, had been dropped behind enemy lines. He had organized the Apuania Partisan Division consisting of five brigades. His headquarters were located near the Serchio Valley. Liaison with him was initially maintained through Major McIntosh and Captain McDermatt, #1 Special Force officers. Subsequently, their functions were taken over by Captain Steven, also of #1 Special Force.

For front line partisan activities, Lieutenant Fermachelli and three enlisted men from the United States OSS were attached to the Division. He was subsequently replaced by Captain Manzani, and additional enlisted men were

The 92nd Division Pack Battalion (Provisional) and its mules were essential in the mountainous spine of Italy with its limited trails and footpaths. Mules could carry ammunition and rations to almost inaccessible areas. The 92nd Division Pack Battalion (Provisional) was manned by Italians. (Opposite page, also.)

assigned. Their efforts resulted in the organization of two partisan companies. One company of 180 partisans operated in the Coastal sector and another of 250 partisans operated in the Serchio Valley. Platoons of these companies were located close to but behind hostile front lines. One OSS enlisted man was in charge of the activities of each platoon.

Partisan activities provided information on enemy activities in their rear areas; supplied a safe channel for repatriation of ex-POWs, crashed Allied airmen, refugees, friendly agents, and friendly patrols; as well as disrupted hostile supplies and communications. Enemy forces were compelled to divert combat troops from the front to protect supply lines and rear installations. It soon became apparent that all prisoners of war, both friend and foe, talked. Accordingly, insofar as possible, knowledge of operational plans were limited to those with a need to know. The 92nd Division's chief interrogator was a small U.S. German-Jewish Captain. His modus operandi was to confine a stubborn German in a basement of a building, used for the purpose, with a map of Northern Italy on the wall, a civilian suit on a rack, and a loaded 45-caliber pistol on the table. After reminding the prisoner of what the Germans were doing to the Jews, he would say "Your only chance is to grab that pistol, kill me, and try to escape. Otherwise, I am going to kill you, put you in those civilian clothes, and report that I have executed a spy." On occasion, the 92nd Division captured a number of female spies, including, in the last days of the war, "Axis Sally." Women were forced to talk by making them stand in a corner of a brightly lighted room in the presence of male interrogators. After a number of hours, they talked.

The 92nd Division was now deployed with the 365th Infantry on the coastal plains, the 371st Infantry (less the 3rd Battalion), in the foothills just west of the coastal sector, and the 370th Infantry, with the 3rd Battalion, 371st Infantry attached, in the Serchio Valley. At 0700 on 16 November, the 370th Infantry launched an attack to capture Castelnuovo, a key road and rail center in the Serchio Valley, and the high ground dominating it. The 3rd Battalion, 371st Infantry, moved forward against light resistance, seized Grottorotondo, and remained there until the end of the day.

The attack of the 1st Battalion, in the center of the 370th Infantry sector, was to capture the mountain villages of Eglio and Sassi. The plan envisioned an assault of the mountain by the 1st Battalion from the south concurrently with an assault from the north by partisans. In anticipation of the partisan effort a three-aeroplane (C-47) drop of shoes, arms, ammunitions, and medical supplies had been made a few days before. The enemy became aware of these intentions and conducted a *Rastellamente* (gathering up) in the partisan-held hills. This scattered the partisan forces and rendered them ineffective so that their attack was not successful. Meanwhile, the 1st Battalion encountered extremely strong resistance and by nightfall had been unable to make any

In the Serchio Valley, we went forward on the attack through an olive grove. (Note the small stone walls that made a terrace around each tree and the denuded state of the trees here from battlefield fire.)

. . . And we took a few prisoners. (Here Germans emerge from cover escorted by an American infantryman.)

gains.

The 3rd Battalion, on the right of the Serchio Valley, was successful in reaching the mountain town of Lama. However, heavy enemy mortar and artillery fire forced them to abandon the town. The offensive was resumed on the morning of 17 November. The 3rd Battalion, 371st Infantry, moved forward towards Mount d'Anima. L Company was caught in a draw at the base of the hill by extremely intense hostile heavy mortar and machine gun fire. Lt. Magellan C. Mars was killed, and half of his company were either killed or wounded. The attack was brought to a halt.

Efforts of the other two assault battalions of the 370th Infantry also proved unsuccessful in the face of determined hostile resistance supported by effective machine gun, mortar, and artillery fire. On 18 November, the leading elements of the Regiment were directed to reorganize and consolidate their positions. The Regiment had advanced about three to four miles. However, Castelnuovo had not been captured. In the meantime, in the center of the Division Zone, the 371st Infantry was deployed with its 1st Battalion on the right and the 2nd Battalion on the left. The Regiment's activities were characterized by strong patrols and platoon and company attacks.

On 8 November, the 1st Battalion was successful in moving forward against relatively light resistance and clearing Azzano, Bosati, Terrinca, and Leviglini. However, Mount Cauala, in the 2nd Battalion zone of action, dominated the area, and hostile artillery fire made daylight movement precarious. Enemy machine gunners, in caves on Mount Cauala, made resupply and communications over the Pietrasanta-Seravezza road very difficult.

On 15 November, a 2nd Battalion patrol moved halfway up Mount Cauala without encountering enemy resistance. The patrol was reinforced by a platoon and then an entire company. The company dug in for the night in anticipation of moving up the mountain the next morning. During the night, mortar fire fell on their positions, but the mortars were silenced by friendly artillery. The next day every movement was met with hostile mortar fire. The troops spent the next two days holding on to their positions without any gains. The following day, 18 November, at 1430, following a 15-minute preparation by all available artillery, 2nd Lt. Royal L. Bolling, with his platoon, moved up the rugged slope. The climb was exhausting. Casualties mounted. Lieutenant Bolling, his platoon sergeant, and two riflemen finally reached the top and found themselves in a fierce hand-to-hand fight. Two of the Americans were killed. Lieutenant Bolling and one soldier withdrew taking two Polish prisoners with them. Mount Cauala was not taken, the company withdrew from its side, and the battalion resumed its patrolling activities.

General Almond visited and flew over the front-line elements almost daily. On one occasion, while he and a small party were on their way to visit the 2nd Battalion, 371st Infantry, on Mount Cauala, they came under hostile artillery

Following the assault, appropriate decorations were awarded. (See opposite also.)

fire while traveling on the Pietrasanta-Seravezza road. The party took cover in the roadside ditch. General Almond crawled in one direction; his aide 1st Lt. Jesse Wooten, the other. Lieutenant Wooten was killed when hit by a German 88-mm shell.

The presence of Polish troops in German units prompted the use of front-line broadcasts to persuade them to desert. Public address systems with loudspeakers close to hostile front lines were employed to deliver the messages. Sometimes these speakers were mounted on tanks and sometimes

(TRANSLATION)

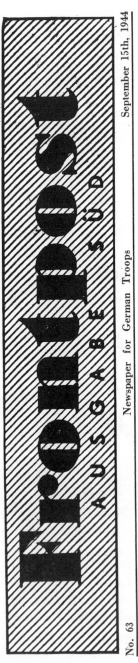

Front|post

AUSGABE SÜD

No. 63   Newspaper for German Troops   September 15th, 1944

Aachen under shell-fire

New American Army on the Western Front

On September 14th Aachen came under fire from 155 mm guns of the American 1st Army. Units of this army had on this day crossed the German frontier on a front of 15 kilometres and to a depth of 12 kilometres, had penetrated into positions of the Westwall north of Luxemburg, had liberated nearly the whole of the Duchy and had made another penetration into

zaire were still holding out on September 14th.

It has been disclosed hat there is now a sixth Allied Army on the Western Front — the American 9th Army, under Lt.-General Simpson. Its present position has not yet been announced.

So far more than half a million German soldiers have been taken prisoner

Warsaw suburb captured

On September 14th the 1st Byelo-Russian Army, with which the Polish 1st Infantry Division is fighting, took Praga, the big suburb of Warsaw east of the Vistula.

Advancing on East Prussia from the south, the 2nd Byelo-Russian Army took the German fortress of Lomza, 30 kilometres from the German frontier, on September 13th, and on the following day Novogrod. Moscow reports that in this area the Germans had established the most formidable defences that the Red Army had ever

Germany north of Trier.

West and north west of Aachen, Allied troops have crossed into Holland near Maastricht. On September 15th the OKW reported: «Between Maastricht and Aachen the North Americans, with the support of strong armoured formations, continued their offensive. Maastricht was lost.»

Farther north, the British 2nd Army cleared the Germans from a long stretch of the Albert Canal and crossed the Scheldt Canal. In the coastal area, the Canadian 1st Army took Bruges.

In Lorraine, the American 3rd Army continued to extend its bridgeheads over the Moselle south of Metz and took Thionville.

Striking up from Southern France, the Allied 7th Army joined up with the American 3rd Army and advanced on the Burgundian Gate.

Far in the rear of the Allied advance, the German garrison of Le Havre, after undergoing on September 12th an air-attack in which RAF heavy bombers dropped 5,500 tons of bombs, surrendered on September 13th to the Canadian 1st Army. The garrisons of Dunkirk, Calais, Boulogne, and of the Breton ports, Brest, Lorient and St. Na-

in the West this summer — including 320,000 by the American 1st and 3rd Armies, nearly 80,000 by the Allied 7th Army, over 70,000 by the British 1st Army and about 53,000 by the partisans of the French Army of the Interior. This last figure includes 18,000 cut-off Germans who surrendered in a body to the partisans south of Orleans on September 12th.

encountered.

In Southern Poland, the 1st Ukrainian Army has taken Krosno, near the Czechoslovakian frontier.

In the Balkans, the 3rd Ukrainian Army has continued its occupation of Bulgaria. The 2nd Ukrainian Army has made contact in Eastern Serbia with units of the Yugoslav People's Army, and is advancing rapidly through Northern Transylvania in the direction of Hungary.

Psychological Warfare.

they were placed in foxholes. These speakers invariably drew hostile artillery fire. 1st Lt. Alfred D. Sieminski broadcast, in Polish and German, both news items and promise of food and safe conduct through the lines. During the broadcasts, front-line commanders held their fire, and a ten-minute smoke screen was laid down. On 22 November, following the instructions of Lieutenant Sieminski, six POW's immediately deserted and 25 others followed during the next few hours.

As another form of psychological warfare, leaflets aimed at lowering the morale and will to resist were disseminated by means of artillery shells and aircraft. These leaflets included the long-range strategical "FRONTPOST" and other material that discussed the situation in Germany, tactical leaflets designed to meet the given tactical situation on the 92nd Division front, and safe conduct passes. Hostile forces responded with propaganda leaflets. They apparently had no effect on our personnel. Activities by the 365th Infantry on the coast were primarily limited to patrolling.

In order to provide much needed rest for certain of its units, as a part of its plan for regrouping in preparation for resumption of the offensive in December, Fifth Army anticipated withdrawing certain elements of the 92nd Division. In late November, the 92nd Division was alerted to provide a regimental combat team for Fifth Army use. General Almond selected the 365th Infantry for this assignment. It was the least committed regiment at that time. In addition to the 365th Infantry, the combat team included the 597th Field Artillery Battalion, B Company, 317th Engineer (C) Battalion, and A Company, 317th Medical Battalion.

On 30 November, the 3rd Battalion, 371st Infantry, relieved the 365th Infantry of its responsibility for the coastal sector extending from the coast to Highway 1. The 3rd Battalion, 371st Infantry, was placed under direct control of the 92nd Division. The 365th Regimental Combat Team moved to the 88th Division sector and attached to II Corps on 3 December. Subsequently, the 3rd Battalion, 370th Infantry, moved to the 6th South African Armored Division sector and was attached to IV Corps. The 2nd Battalion, 370th Infantry, moved to the 1st Brazilian Division sector and was also attached to IV Corps. The 370th Infantry was left with only one of its own battalions.

In response to the comment by the Assistant Chief of Staff G-3, 92nd Division, that these moves would detract from the Division's ability to hold its broad (23-mile) front, a Fifth Army staff officer stated that the moves were essential even if it meant leaving a part of the front line uncovered. However, Fifth Army's concern about the 92nd Division's ability to hold its end of the line prompted the assignment to the Division of the 366th Infantry Regiment. [4]

Col. H. D. Queen's all-black 366th Infantry Regiment had been employed, by battalion, as air base security. The Regiment was assembled and brought to Leghorn on 26 November. Although it had passed its combat firing tests and

Hostile Psychological Warfare. Both sides expended considerable resources, time, and effort in attempting to lower the morale of soldiers on the opposing forces and encouraging them to desert. These are examples of German leaflets fired into the 92nd's lines. The soldier is smiling in the picture because as a German prisoner, he no longer has to fight.

Why is he smiling?

LIFE

NOVEMBER 1944 10 CENTS
YEARLY SUBSCRIPTION $4.50

Hostile Psychological Warfare.

SAFE CONDUCT

The American colored soldier who is presenting this certificate *has ceased to fight.*
He is to be removed at once from the combat area. He is
to be well looked after and to receive food and medical
attention as required.

TRANSLATION: **PASSIERSCHEIN**
ÜBERSETZUNG:

**Der amerikanische Negersoldat, der diesen Passierschein
vorzeigt, *hat den Kampf eingestellt.*
Er ist sofort aus dem Kampfgebiet zu entfernen und gut zu
behandeln. Er hat Anspruch auf Verpflegung und wenn nötig
auf ärztliche Behandlung.**

15 company grade officers had attended a three-week leadership and battle training course, its overall state of training and operational readiness had suffered as a result of its dispersed and prolonged security guard duty. Morale was high, though, in anticipation of its combat assignment.

Within the 92nd Division, except when actually in combat with the enemy, training was habitual in reserve regiments, battalions, companies, and to some extent in reserve platoons. Each regiment of the Division was assigned an area in the Division training area. A complete tent camp was erected to expedite the early beginning of training for reserve battalions as they were rotated out of the line. New units, attached to the Division, were given refresher training before entering combat.

The 366th Infantry Regiment was attached to the 92nd Division on 28 November and moved to the Division training area. Colonel Queen felt that three months of intensive training would prepare his regiment for combat duty. While it was agreed that an intensive training period in the Division training area was desirable, the exigencies of the situation dictated that the regiment be employed as soon as practical. Accordingly, a training program, which included battle indoctrination by attaching small units to those of the division in the line, was developed. In the implementation of this plan, elements were attached and fed into the line as follows:

On 30 November, E Company was attached to the 3rd Battalion, 371st Infantry, on the coast.

On 1 December, the Intelligence and Reconnaissance Platoon was attached to the 92nd Reconnaissance Platoon.

On 2 December, the 2nd Battalion (less E Company) was moved to the Serchio Valley and attached to the 370th Infantry.

On 5 December, I Company was also moved to the Serchio Valley and attached to the 370th Infantry.

On 9 December, the Cannon Company and Anti-Tank Company were attached to the 371st Infantry.

On 11 December, K Company was moved to the Serchio Valley and attached to the 370th Infantry.

On 12 December, the 1st Battalion relieved the 3rd Battalion, 371st Infantry, on the coast and under the operational direction of the 92nd Division, and assumed responsibility for the left of the Division front from the coast to Highway 1.

On 14 December, the Regimental Headquarters was moved to the vicinity of Forte dei Marmi and assigned responsibility for its 1st Battalion and the coastal sector.

The 3rd Battalion (less K Company) remained in the Division training area in Division Reserve.

Initially, the 92nd Cavalry Reconnaissance Troop was employed in its traditional role of scouting and patrolling to protect the Division's right flank. Subsequently, its mission was to occupy the approximately 8,000-yard center portion of the division's front in extremely rugged mountain terrain.

On the night of 14 December, the Forte dei Marmi area was subjected to heavy concentrations of hostile artillery fire from coastal guns at La Spezia. The next morning Colonel Queen reported to the Division Commander that his health would not permit the rigors of combat and that he was reporting to the hospital. He could not be deferred by persuasion or threats. Lt. Colonel Ferguson, the Regimental Executive Officer, although apparently lacking in command experience, assumed command of the Regiment.

During the month of November, there were a total of 71 killed in action in the 92nd Division and its attachments, and there were 286 wounded and 153 missing in action.

RESUMPTION OF THE ATTACK

On 28 November, Field Marshal Alexander, Commander-in-Chief A.A.I. (15th Army Group) directed the preparation of an offensive to break through the Apennine defenses. Eighth Army was to continue the operation to drive the enemy west of Santerno and secure bridgeheads over the river. Fifth Army was to be prepared to resume the offensive, with the main thrust on Bologna, on three days notice from 7 December. Its plan was to attack on the axis of Highway 65 with the II Corps making the main effort. One regiment of the 88th Division would be in Army reserve. The 92nd Division would maintain pressure on the enemy in the coastal sector and maintain contact with IV Corps on its right.

The 2nd Battalion, 370th Infantry, was attached to the Task Force 45 on the left of the IV Corps. The 365th Regimental Combat Team was attached to the 88th Division, on the right of the II Corps line, and moved to its new position on 3 December. The 3rd Battalion, 370th Infantry, moved to the east, where it was attached to the 6th South African Armored Division on the right of the IV Corps line.

The remaining elements of the 92nd Division were deployed as follows. On the left, from the coast to Highway No. 1, was the 366th Infantry with one battalion, the 1st Battalion. It was supported by a company of the 751st Tank Battalion, a company of the 894th Tank Destroyer Battalion, and the 600th Field Artillery Battalion (less A Battery). In the center position was the 371st Infantry with its 1st, 2nd and 3rd Battalion on the line supported by the 599th Field Artillery Battalion, with the Cannon Company attached, the 894th Tank Destroyer Battalion, the 71st and 76th (British) Heavy Anti-Aircraft Regiments, and the 751st Tank Battalion. The 370th Infantry was in the Serchio Valley with its 1st Battalion on the left at Gallicano and the 2nd Battalion, 366th Infantry, on the right at Barga supported by the 598th Field Artillery

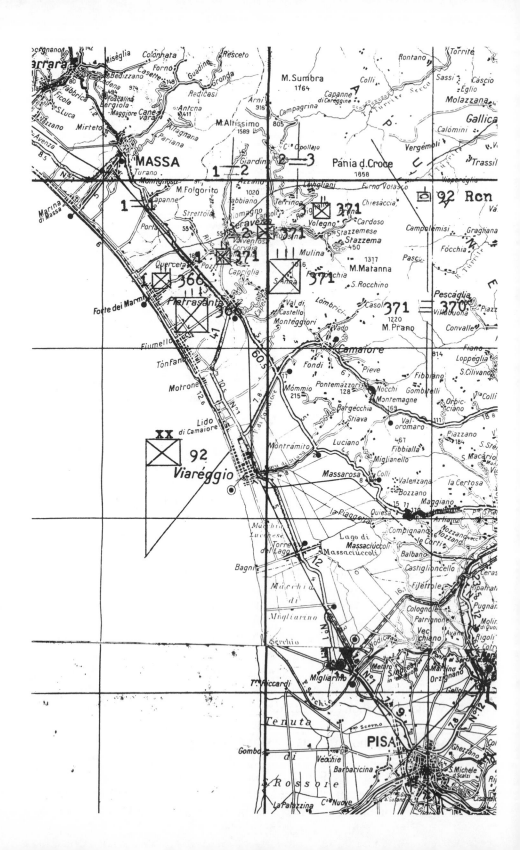

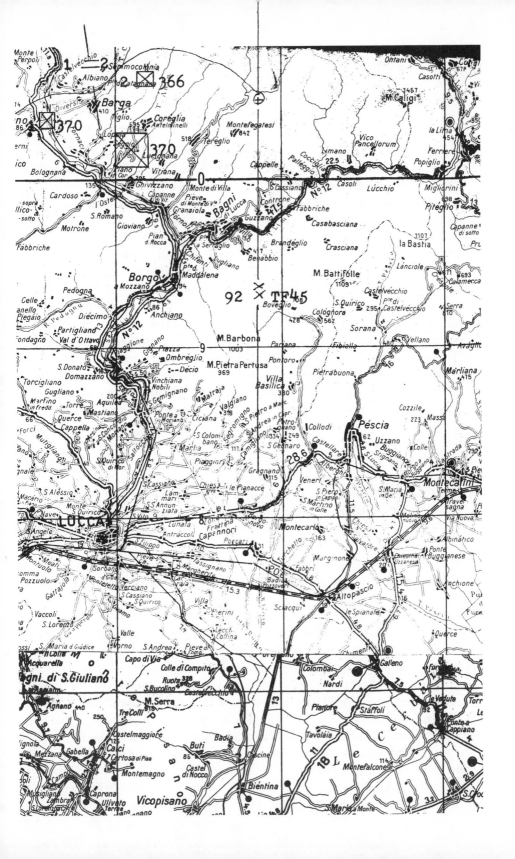

Battalion, with the 366th and 370th Cannon Companies attached, and A Battery, 600th Field Artillery Battalion.

By the second week of December, the British Army attack, while making steady progress, had not reached the advanced stage that had been planned as a condition preceding the launch of the Fifth Army attack. The weather all along the front became increasingly worse, making offensive operation well-nigh impossible. By 7 December, the British Army had captured Ravenna and was pushing on to the Lanone River, but that river and the Serio River were to be crossed before the enemy could be driven west of the Santerno River. The Fifth Army attack, therefore, was postponed from day to day until the weather improved and the progress of the Eighth Army could bring about conditions required for the Fifth Army to launch its attack with any assurance of success.

In early December an analysis of ammunition stocks indicated that sufficient supplies were on hand to support a 15-day attack during December, but such consumption would result in inability to carry out further offensive action until after 28 January 1945. By that time, receipt of scheduled allocations would again boost the dump supply to a point which would allow full artillery support to any operation. Allotments of ammunition were greatly reduced. Limitations of 15 rounds per day for each 105-mm howitzer, 18 rounds per day per 155-mm howitzer, and 11 rounds per day per 155-mm gun were imposed initially. Later in the winter, the allocations were further reduced. Drastic cuts were also made in infantry-supporting ammunition. These were initially applied to 81-mm and later 60-mm mortar.

As a result of this shortage of supporting ammunition and with the purpose of utilizing all available weapons to inflict casualties and harass the enemy, Lt. Colonel Arnold, the Assistant Chief of Staff G-3, developed a plan for offensive fire known as "Infantry Weapon Shoots." The plan was approved by General Almond and ordered into effect on 12 December. All heavy weapons that had unrestricted ammunition allowance were organized, placed under the control of the Assistant Chief of Staff G-3, and employed to relieve the artillery of its responsibilities for harassing and interdiction (H&I) fires. These weapons included 40-mm anti-aircraft guns (firing tracer ammunition), .50-caliber machine guns (with tracer ammunition, 57-mm anti-tank guns (firing solid projectiles), and 37-mm tank guns.

The weapons were placed in forward areas in order to maximize their range capabilities. Based on information provided by the Assistant Chief of Staff G-2, and recommendations provided by subordinate headquarters, concentrated fire on specific targets at prescribed times was directed by Division Headquarters. The concentration of effort served to maximize effectiveness and the coordination of timing to minimize enemy reaction. Thus, it was extremely difficult for the enemy to locate and neutralize 8 to 10 batteries of .50-caliber machine guns, spread across the entire front, when they all began

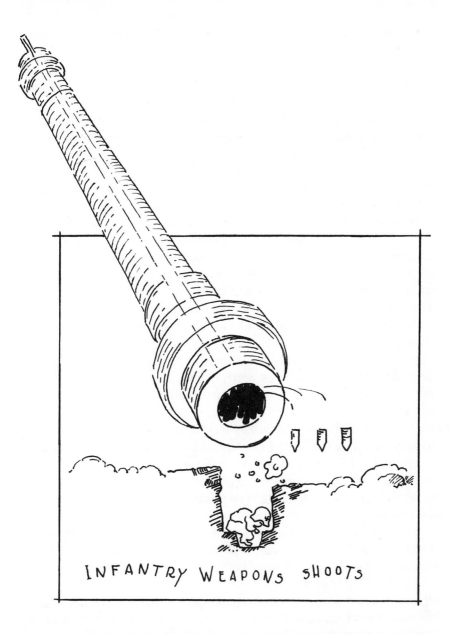

INFANTRY WEAPONS SHOOTS

In order to conserve artillery ammunition, in short supply, concentrated fire of least used infantry weapons was used for harrassing and interdiction missions.

to fire simultaneously. Conversely, the fire from the 40-mm anti-aircraft guns, firing tracers, almost always brought hostile artillery fire. However, most of the time it took 20 minutes for enemy artillery to react. Consequently, after completing a five-minute shoot, the 40-mm anti-aircraft weapons always had ten minutes to vacate their positions and move to alternate locations.

The directive assigning targets and prescribing time of fire was promulgated by the Assistant Chief of Staff G-3, in overlay form as an attachment to the daily Operation Instructions. Initially, the "shoots" were held for five minutes every half hour during the 24-hour period. Later, it was decided to reduce this expenditure so that the number of concentrations were limited to approximately 15 to 20 during the 24-hour period.

The "shoots" made it possible to harass enemy areas close to the front while artillery ammunition was reserved for areas deep in hostile territory. In view of the extended front and the limited artillery ammunition, harassing fire by the artillery could not be concentrated sufficiently to produce the desired effect. It was felt that within their range and trajectory limitations, the 40-mm anti-aircraft guns, .50-caliber machine guns, 57-mm anti-tank guns, and 37-mm tank guns could fulfill the mission equally well, especially since ammunition for these weapons had been expended only in very limited quantities previously, and its expenditure was not restricted. Additionally, the employment offered an opportunity for increased efficiency of the crews serving these weapons.

The weapons were employed in batteries of 2 to 4 guns each. Batteries were dug in, and shelter and foxholes were provided for crew members. Alternate positions were selected. Telephone communications from battery positions to companies or battalions were installed. At first, the gun crews were very reluctant to fire. However, after they learned that the enemy usually did not retaliate, except in the case of the 40-mm anti-aircraft guns, the reluctance disappeared and firing increased, both in volume and in effectiveness. The crews of the .50-caliber machine guns became so proficient that they could put the first burst of fire in the slits of hostile machine gun positions at a range of 1,000 yards.

Daily reports were submitted to Division Headquarters as to the number of weapons in position, the number of weapons in reserve, the amount of ammunition expended, and targets engaged. This information was consolidated and published in overlay form as an enclosure to the daily G-3 Periodic Report. A monthly consolidated report was published which also included totals of ammunition issued and ammunition expended. As a result of these "infantry weapon shoots," enemy movement decreased in the forward areas, and enemy patrols were less active than before. Prisoners of war reported that the "shoots" were not only casualty-producing but also were very demoralizing, and in some cases caused them to withdraw from some of their most forward blocking positions.

Several major changes in the Allied Command occurred in mid-December. British Marshal Wilson relinquished his command of the Mediterranean

Plans, when approved and ordered executed verbally, were always confirmed by written Field Orders. After promulgation, changes or modifications were directed by means of Operation Instructions issued to a particular field order.

Theater to Marshal Alexander. On 16 December, while Fifth Army was resting and refitting its forces for a renewal of the offensive, Gen. Mark Clark left his Fifth Army Headquarters at Futa Pass to take command of 15th Army Group. His place was filled by Lt. Gen. Lucian K. Truscott, Jr.

On 17 December, in Field Order No. 4, General Almond directed the 92nd Division to attack to seize limited objectives. B Company, 371st Infantry, launched an attack to capture Pian di Lago which apparently caught the Germans off guard. However, the alarm spread rapidly and soon the hillside was alive with mortar and machine gun fire. Although hindered by steep terrain and determined enemy resistance, B Company managed to fight its way up Pian di Lago until it reached the crest where hostile resistance and mountain casualties were such that further advance could not be made. Under the cover of artillery fire, the company withdrew to a more covered position. On the coast, activities were limited to patrols by the 1st Battalion, 366th Infantry, along the Cinquale Canal.

On 18 December, the 2nd Battalion, 370th Infantry, was released from control of Task Force 45 and returned to its parent unit in the Serchio Valley. An attack designed to secure Lama di Soto ridge was planned for Christmas morning. Rumors of a possible German assault persisted. Enemy patrols began to enter the Division area more frequently, especially in the Serchio Valley. An enemy deserter reported that his unit, a part of the Italia Division, had moved to the front of the 92nd Division shortly before 19 December. Civilians coming through the lines reported the Germans to be feverishly rebuilding the bridges and repairing the roads they had previously blown in the western area. This was confirmed by aerial photographs.

Both hostile and friendly forces became more alert, and the taking of German prisoners came to a halt. Pressure by both Fifth Army and 92nd Division on front-lint units to take prisoners began to mount. Larger and larger power patrols to take prisoners were dispatched without success. Finally the 371st Infantry reported that K Company had taken a prisoner. The Division was directed not to take the time to interrogate him but immediately to evacuate him to Fifth Army POW cage.

The Assistant Chief of Staff G-3 was anxious to learn what method K Company had used to take a prisoner successfully. On close interrogation of K Company Commander, he found that in order to prevent further casualties in an effort to take prisoners, the Commander had given the company's Italian KP a bag of K rations and sent him to the German lines to persuade one of them to surrender. The Italian and German had worked together several months before on building the German positions. That is how Fifth Army took a prisoner on that day. However, very little was learned from that prisoner. A few days later a priest came through the 370th Infantry lines and stated that the Germans were going to attack in the Serchio Valley on Christmas day. The Division's efforts to confirm this report were unsuccessful.

Another indication of a possible attack was the build-up of enemy forces in the western section which greatly exceeded the ordinary defensive require- ments of that flank. In addition to the Monte Rosa and San Marco Italian Divisions and two regiments of the 148th Grenadier Division that had been opposing the 92nd Division for some time, the German 157th Mountain Division, which had been heading for Northeastern Italy, was turned around in the middle of its journey on 15 December and dispatched to the La Spezia area. The third regiment, the 285th, of the 148th German Grenadier Division was brought down from Genoa. The Italia Division, purportedly ready for employment in the counterattack role in support of German units, which had been previously concentrated in the Parma area, was moving to the La Spezia area. Recent reliefs on other parts of the German Army Group front made it possible for two additional divisions, currently in reserve, to be used in conjunction with any projected offensive. These were the 16th SS Panzer Grenadier Division and the 26th Panzer Division. Also the possibility of the

Men of the 370th Infantry take cover from hostile machine gun fire. This shot by a combat photographer appeared in *The Buffalo*, 92nd Infantry Division weekly paper. It shows three infantrymen behind an armored personnel carrier of the 1st Armored Division in combat gear. They are armed with M-1 rifles. The man at the center is aiming his weapon, while the one kneeling rifleman prepares to fire.

5th Mountain Division being used for this purpose could not be altogether discounted.

In evaluating the buildup of forces in the western sector, U.S. forces granted the enemy the capability of launching an offensive with a force of five divisions. This capability could not be ignored. The only force between this enemy threat and the Fifth Army supply base of Leghorn was the thinly-held line of the 92nd Division.

The 370th Anti-Tank Company, trained in infantry tactics, was equipped with rifles, light machine guns, and Browning automatic rifles in addition to its organic antitank weapons. It was assigned to a blocking position in the vicinity of Vergemoli, on the Regiment's left flank. In the early dawn of 22 December the company was hit by a German power patrol of company size. Fighting became intense. Lt. Col. John J. Phelan, the Regimental Executive Officer, was present in order to bolster the defense of the company. The fighting developed into hand-to-hand conflict. Suddenly, a number of the Germans started fighting other Germans. When the fighting subsided and the hostile forces withdrew, the 370th Anti-Tank Company found that they had a platoon of 16 Russians, in German uniforms, who had changed sides. These men proved to be very valuable in pointing out mine fields and other obstacles. The Regiment requested that they be allowed to stay and fight with them. However, Fifth Army insisted that they be evacuated to their POW cage. From there they were turned over to the Soviet Liaison Officer who had them all executed. When Italy surrendered to the Allies in 1943 and declared war on Germany, elements of the Italian Army, north of the German line were assembled, reorganized into division size units similar to German Grenadier divisions, trained under German supervision, and intergrated into General Kesselring's Armies. After his rescue, Mussolini was the titular Commander-in-Chief of the Italian Army in the North.

On 23 December, the first heavy snowfall of the winter blanketed the Serchio Valley. The attack planned for Christmas day, against Lama di Sotto, was canceled, and only usual patrol and artillery fire were conducted. The 92nd Division reverted from an offensive posture to that of defense.

92ND DIVISION ON THE DEFENSE

Although Fifth Army's II Corps attack had been tentatively set for Christmas night, it was determined that the left flank of Fifteenth Army Group had to be strengthened. Accordingly, on 23 December, General Clark approved the Fifth Army Commander's plan of allotting reserves to bolster both IV Corps and the 92nd Division. The IV Corps and the 92nd Division were directed to hold their present positions at all cost, to intensify patrolling, and to make maximum improvement of their existing defensive positions.

On 24 December, Maj. Claire S. Curtis' 760th (Medium) Tank Battalion and Col. Oliver W. Hughes' 337th Regimental Combat Team, 85th Division, was attached to the 92nd Division. In addition to those forces, Lt. Col. Forrest E. Love's 84th Chemical Battalion, the 755th Tank Battalion, the 75th 155-mm howitzer and the 530th 155-mm gun American field artillery battalions and two regiments (battalions), the 10th and 17th Medium Regiments, Royal Artillery, of British 5.5-inch guns were moved to the vicinity of Lucca and subsequently attached to the 92nd Division. The 19th and 20th Indian Brigades (Gurkhas and Sikhs) of the 8th Indian Division were placed under the operational control of the 92nd Division and moved into the Serchio Valley. The 6th South African Armored Division reverted to Army control and was directed to be prepared to reinforce the 92nd Division. At about 0200 on 25 December, two tall, handsome officers in British uniforms with red tabs came into the Assistant Chief of Staff G-3's office, stomped their feet, saluted, and said, "We are not British, you know." Lt. Colonel Arnold replied that he did not know; whereupon they replied, "No, we are South Africans." It was most important to them that there be no mistake. The 6th South African Armored Division was the only division the South Africans had. It started as the 1st South African Armored Division. Each time it was pulled out of the line, due to heavy casualties, and reorganized, it was redesignated with the next number. Maj. Gen. W. H. E. Poole, CB, DSO, not only commanded the

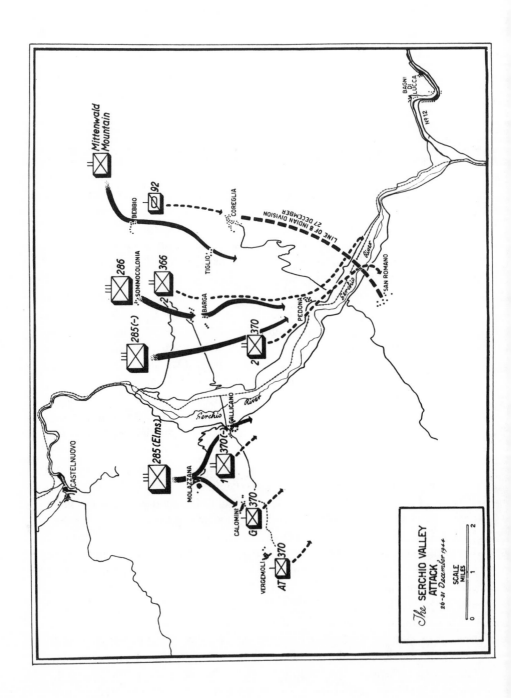

The SERCHIO VALLEY
ATTACK
26-31 December 1944

SCALE
MILES
0   1   2

division in the line, but also the line of communications back to South Africa and the home defenses of South Africa. They were exceptionally good troops.

The fact that the German commanders were fully aware of the situation in the 370th Infantry sector was demonstrated in a postwar interrogation by Lt. Colonel Arnold when Brig. General Fretter Pico, commanding General of the 148th (German) Grenadier Division, said, "The weaknesses of your deployment in the Serchio Valley in December 1944 were that your troops were deployed on a front which was too long for the number of troops available, and your reserves were too far in the rear area which prevented their being deployed immediately."

The enemy launched a predawn attack on 26 December following a series of probing thrusts by patrols the previous night. The enemy struck the 92nd Division at several points in the rugged mountains, on a six-mile front astride the Serchio River. The attack was preceded by a very heavy mortar barrage and about 800 rounds of artillery fire. It was accompanied by a marked increase of artillery fire in the coastal sector, although no appreciable increase in ground action developed there.

West of the Serchio River, elements of the German 2nd Battalion, 285th Grenadier Regiment, 148th Grenadier Division, and the Brescia, Alpine, Battalion of the Italian Monta Rosa Division struck the 1st Battalion, 370th Infantry, near Molazzana, four miles south of Castelnuovo, and G Company, 2nd Battalion, 370th Infantry, at Calomini, south and west of Molazzana. East of the river, large elements, identified as belonging to the 2nd Battalion, 285th Grenadier Regiment, and 2nd Battalion, 286th Grenadier Regiment, 148th Grenadier Division, attacked the village of Sommocolonia held by two platoons of E Company, 366th Infantry. Hand-to-hand fighting in the street developed. The enemy was estimated to be attacking in strength of about one reinforced regiment on each side of the river in the initial assault.

Early in the day, the Germans infiltrated the town of Calomini, held by G Company, 370th Infantry. At the same time A and C Companies, 370th Infantry, in Molazzana were struck. By 1400, G Company had been driven from Calomini. The 1st Battalion, 370th Infantry, also gave ground, although fighting on the west side of the river died down considerably.

Late in the morning, the Germans redirected the force of their main attack on the Division's right flank by hitting the Sommocolonia-Bebbio area with the 4th Mountain Battalion and the Austro-German Mittenwald Battalion, both high mountain troops. Pouring down the sheltered draws between Bebbio and Scarpello, led by Italian guides familiar with the area, over 200 Germans of the Mittenwald Battalion split a platoon of the 92nd Reconnaissance Troop, overrunning the American positions in the areas and completely outflanking the entire 370th Infantry line. The Reconnaissance Troop was ordered to withdraw the prepared positions near Coreglia.

Clearing refugees from the road in order to bring up reinforcements. All armies had the problem of refugees and displaced persons cluttering the narrow European roads when they wished to move. Sometimes, as here, the MPs could be brutal about clearing the way by simply tipping the carts and barrows off of the road to let vital military traffic cross a narrow spot such as this gulley or bomb crater bridged by the Engineers with a PSP roadway.

Bitter fighting continued meanwhile at Sommocolonia where the Germans were endeavoring to roll up the 370th Infantry line, and the besieged troops of the 366th Infantry were striving to drive the Germans from the village. The deterioration of the situation prompted Lt. Graham H. Jenkins to request reinforcements. At 0735, the 2nd Battalion, 370th Infantry, ordered a platoon of E Company there. Fighting from door to door continued. Lt. John Fox, Cannon Company, 366th Infantry, as forward observer for the 598th Field Artillery Battalion, with E Company, 366th Infantry, adjusted close in supporting fires and finally, deliberately, brought the artillery fire on his own position, killing himself and the surrounding Germans. At 1145, the forces in Sommocolonia were ordered to withdraw. Remnants of E Company, 366th Infantry, managed to fight their way through the fast-closing escape route, falling back to Barga Ridge. Only 17 of 60 men managed to escape from the town. The others were killed or wounded in the battle for the village.

Before noon, G Company, 366th Infantry, having suffered many casualties and being badly disorganized, fell back leaving a gap of about 500 yards along the east bank of the river, which the Germans exploited almost immediately. Rushing an unopposed infantry company into the gap, the enemy moved rapidly southward toward the now uncovered road to Barga. The loss of this position forced other elements of the 2nd Battalion, 366th Infantry, to give further ground to avoid being outflanked. The command post of the 370th Infantry and the advance command post of the 92nd Division at Gallicano were threatened. Lt. Col. John J. Phelan, Regimental Executive Officer, rounded up every available man in the area to meet the threat. C Battery commander, 598th Field Artillery Battalion, gave the order, "Target that column of Germans advancing to our front; continuous fire." Three tanks were also directed to fire on the advancing enemy. Colonel Sherman reported the situation to General Almond and stated, "I have dug in my cooks and clerks around my command post and we are prepared to stay here until the end." General Almond ordered him to move to a new position further to the rear. F Company, 370th Infantry, which had been preparing secondary positions west of the Serchio River, was hurriedly moved across the river to fill the gap caused by the collapse of G Company, 366th Infantry.

The 1st Battalion, 370th Infantry, after losing Molazzana, fell back and took up position a mile northwest of Gallicano. However, G Company, 366th Infantry, withdrew further to the rear under heavy enemy shelling, uncovering the right flank of the 1st Battalion, 370th Infantry, thus causing it to fall back to conform to the new line established by elements of the 366th Infantry.

The 370th Infantry, sure that it could stand fast, asked that a motorized battalion of the 19th Indian Brigade be used on its right flank to prevent further encirclement. There was some confusion concerning control. When the matter was settled, it was too late to get the troops into position before dark.

Refugees escaping the German attack in the Serchio Valley.

The 19th and 21st Indian Brigades of the 8th Indian Division were eventually released by IV Corps, arrived in the evening, and were attached to the 370th Infantry. They occupied previous reconnoitered positions on the right of the river. On the west side of the river, G Company, 370th Infantry, reoccupied many of its former positions.

To prevent the enemy attack from developing into any further threat to the supply base at Leghorn, the Fifth Army winter offensive to capture Bologna was postponed. The 1st Armored Division was ordered out of the line on II Corps front and sent west to strengthen the defense of Lucca. The 135th Regimental Combat Team, 34th Division, was attached to IV Corps and moved to positions north of Viareggio. The 337th Regimental Combat Team, 85th Division, already attached to the 92nd Division was moved to the Lucca area. The 8th Indian Division moved up behind the 92nd Division.

The attack continued at dawn on 27 December, with the main thrust being the area east of the river between Gallicano and Coreglia. The attack made steady progress against the 2nd Battalion, 366th Infantry, and parts of the 2nd Battalion, 370th Infantry. The 2nd Battalion, 366th Infantry, evacuated Barga during the morning. White-clad German mountain troops occupied Tiglio. The 2nd Battalion, 370th Infantry, with a company of the 19th Indian Brigade attached, moved to the east to cover the threat. Small thrusts were made west of the river around Molazzana. However, the situation remained stable all during the day, and the enemy made no substantial gains.

The enemy captured two 57-mm guns and turned them against the 366th Infantry, which also lost a number of heavy machine guns. The results were disastrous. By 1300 the 2nd Battalion, 366th Infantry, had fallen back from their second defense line and the Germans had penetrated through the center as far as the Village of Pedona, two miles south of Barga. Lt. Colonel Phelan gathered the disorganized and scattered companies for a final stand. At 1500, the 19th Indian Brigade established a line, behind the 2nd Battalion, 366th Infantry, and the 2nd Battalion, 370th Infantry, from Coreglia to San Romano, a mile south of Pedona.

Maj. Gen. D. Russell, Commanding General, 8th Indian Division, assumed command of the Serchio River Valley sector in mid-afternoon of 27 December. The right boundary of the 92nd Division was moved to the east narrowing its responsibility to the coastal sector. All of the 370th Infantry and attached units on the east side of the river were withdrawn to the west side to positions behind the 1st Battalion. Colonel Sherman's forces were responsible for holding the high ground south of Gallicano with the 8th Indian Division units on their right, across the river.

By 2200, the Germans made contact with Indian patrols. However, the Germans did not press their attack further and did not reach the defensive line established by the 8th Indian Division. Also on this day, the 1125th Armored

German minefield marker. The Germans, in particular, made great use of defensive minefields. They removed the markers as they withdrew.

Field Artillery Battalion, commanded by Lt. Col. Forrest W. Duff, was attached to the 92nd Division.

The next day the enemy began to retire. Indian patrols made only slight contact when they moved forward to probe the German positions. On 29 December, the 8th Indian Division sent patrols to a depth of 350 to 3,500 yards without contact. The village of Barga was found to be clear of enemy force and was occupied by the 6th Lancers on 30 December. By 1 January the 8th Indian Division had regained practically all of the ground east of the river lost in the attack, including Bebbio and Sommocolonia, while the 370th Infantry, on the west of the river, had moved against slight resistance to Gallicano and

Molazzana. The German threat to the Fifth Army supply line no longer existed.

As the threat of further enemy aggression subsided, the 135th Regimental Combat Team, 34th Division, was relieved from attachment to the 92nd Division, and left the sector on 5 January. The 370th Infantry returned to control the 92nd Division. On 10 January, the 92nd Division completed the relief of the Indians and once again assumed command of the wide front that extended from the Ligurian Sea eastward to the eastern slope of the Serchio Valley. The 365th Infantry was detached from II Corps. Upon return to the 92nd Division, it relieved the 370th Infantry east of the Serchio River. The 366th Infantry, minus its 3rd Battalion, relieved the 370th Infantry west of the Serchio River. The 3rd Battalion, 366th Infantry, remained in position in the coastal sector. The 370th Infantry, minus its anti-tank company, moved to a concentration area north of Pietrasanta.

On 28 December, Fifth Army announced postponement of the assault on Bologna and placed all Army troops on a nine-day alert for resumption of offensive operations. The continuing bad weather, the shift in location of Fifth Army troops, and the depleted ammunition stocks forced the postponement of the planned offensive until spring when the troops would be rested and there would be enough ammunition.

What exactly had been the enemy's design in concentrating forces in the western sector at this time and not following up his initial success remained obscure. It was at this same time that the Von Runstedt counteroffensive on the Western Front was at the height of its success. When the attack came in Italy, it was considered that it might very well be a part of a desperate plan of the German High Command to make one supreme all-out effort to inflict, simultaneously, serious setbacks to the Anglo-American armies on both the Western and the Italian fronts, thus gaining time to sow discord between the Western Powers and their Russian ally.

In a postwar interrogation, Brigadier Otto Fretter-Pico, Commanding General 148th (German) Grenadier Division, told Lt. Colonel Arnold, "I stopped my attack in the vicinity of Fornaci because I did not have sufficient force to allow me to push on to Bagni di Lucca or Lucca. The object of my attack was to stop the American attack on Bologna by diverting reserves from that effort. This objective was accomplished."

About the middle of December, Marshal Kesselring, reportedly wounded by a strafing Allied plane, was replaced by Gen. Heinrich Von Vietinghoff. General Vietinghoff, who had been in command of the German Tenth Army, was considered one of the most able enemy commanders. Lt. Gen. Joachim Lemelsen of Fourteenth Army replaced Vietinghoff in directing the more active Tenth Army, which was opposing the advance of the British Eighth Army. During the month of December, the 92nd Division captured 636 prisoners of war and sustained a total of 529 officers and men killed, wounded, and missing in action.

By 10 January, in the 92nd Division sector, the opposing units facing each other were approximately of equal strength. The 148th Grenadier Division was reinforced by the following Italian units: the Berscia Battalion; the Reconnaissance Battalion, Monte Rosa Division; the 2nd Battalion, 6th Marine Regiment, San Marco Division. The 4th Mountain Battalion and the Mittenwald Battalion had been withdrawn.

The 1st Armored Division remained at Lucca in Army reserve. The 6th South African Armored Division continued defense of its sector under direct Army command. The first elements of a major reinforcement for Fifth Army were received on 27 December when the 86th Mountain Infantry, 10th Mountain Division, arrived at Leghorn. The remainder of the Division arrived in Italy in January. On 14 January, a new separate infantry regiment, the 473rd Infantry, was activated from members of anti-aircraft artillery battalions who had been functioning as foot soldiers for approximately six months under Task Force 45 and the 92nd Division. Headquarters and Headquarters Company, 2nd Armored Group, and the 434th, 435th, 532nd and 900th Anti-Aircraft Artillery Automatic Weapons Battalions were disbanded and their personnel used to form the new regiment with an authorized strength of 143 officers, 5 warrant officers, and 3,049 enlisted men. Col. William P. Yarborough was placed in command of the regiment.

Two weeks after its activation the 473rd Infantry began a strenuous schedule of infantry training along lines which previous experience in organizing and training new infantry units had shown to be necessary. In general the work was the same as that prescribed for older infantry regiments in the Army, but as it was comparatively newly-formed, more basic principles were included. Artillery and tank elements were attached to the regiment to provide combined arms training. Intelligence and counterintelligence instruction was stressed.

During the remainder of January and the first few days of February, the 92nd Division (reinforced) and the opposing 148th Grenadier Division (reinforced) sent out patrols to reconnoiter, to get information, to probe, to take prisoners, and to fight. "Stealth" patrols went out to determine the exact location of specified enemy installations, to reconnoiter paths and approaches, and to perform demolitions or cut lanes through wire. While there were numerous stealth patrols, Lt. Vernon C. Baker, Distinguished Service Cross (DSC) winner, performed his duties in stealth patroling in a superb manner until he lost his life on patrol, as a result of errors of others.

"Power" patrols from platoon to battalion strength, supported by tanks, tank destroyers, and artillery, were in effect small-scale attacks. "Power" patrols went out on each battalion or regimental front on an average of every third night. One of the patrols led by Captain Wetlaufer, E Company, 371st Infantry, to capture prisoners moved out in the early afternoon through a wide band of enemy wire to a ridge line that extended generally west of Mount Cauala, east of Highway 1. Approaching a house which was known to be occupied by the enemy, the patrol captured the enemy lookout and proceeded into the house. The remainder of the enemy squad was below ground level in an improvised dugout under the first floor. A machine gun in position by a window on the first floor was unattended. Hearing the patrol, the enemy made an effort to reach the machine gun, but machine gun fire from the patrol as the enemy attempted to emerge from the entrance to the dugout halted their effort. The patrol threw grenades into the dugout and left with a prisoner and the enemy gun. There were no casualties suffered by the patrol, whereas the enemy casualties included four or five killed and one prisoner.

Typical of this period was 8 January. A quiet day generally along the front, it was filled with activity for patrols that operated from front-line battalions. In the 366th area, accurate enemy mortar fire halted three separate attempts of L Company patrol to reconnoiter the coastal road to the mouth of the Cinquale Canal. A patrol of C Company, 371st Infantry, on the northern terraces of Mount Cauala, was dissolved by a single grenade that was tossed at them by a hidden enemy. A patrol from E Company of the same regiment, which had carefully threaded its way around Mount Castiglione, found cleverly-placed trip wires strung in a path leading into enemy territory.

Early on the evening of 10 January, a raiding party from L Company, 366th Infantry, crossed the mouth of the Cinquale Canal and pushed northward up the beach for about 1,500 yards, then it turned inland. Almost at once the raiders ran into mine fields that were protected by wire. Attempts to cut the wire and cross the mined area failed when the enemy reacted with machine gun and mortar fire. The party drew back down the beach and across the canal. The enemy set off flares that kept the raiders from repeating their efforts.

Another patrol from the 366th Infantry probed a short way north on Highway 1, but when it received machine gun fire from enemy positions in the Strettoia hills, it withdrew. Patrols from other regiments on the line made no contact with the enemy that day.

In the early morning hours of 11 January, a ten-man patrol from E Company, 371st Infantry, went out to search a hamlet east of Mount Strettoia that was reported to be used as an observation point by the Germans. Nothing was found in the buildings of the village. Three scouts in the patrol went on to investigate a group of bunkers nearby. The first four of the cave-like emplacements were empty. As the scouts approached the fifth, a German soldier rose suddenly from behind the sand bags and fired his machine gun. His aim was inaccurate; however, before the patrol could take cover and shoot back, the German indicated that he wanted to surrender. The patrol held its fire; then suddenly, two more Germans appeared above the embankment, and all three Germans began to shoot. In an ensuing five-minute fight, the patrol killed all three of the enemy and then pulled back from the bunkers just in time to avoid German mortar shells which came crashing down in the area.

The cold weather and heavy snowfalls now seriously hampered patrol operations in the Serchio Valley. From 15 to 18 January, the sector was very quiet. Hostile batteries fired a few harassing missions each day. However, enemy fire was light. Heavy snowfall increased the difficulty of moving over the rough terrain. Contact with the enemy was hampered by the enemy's desire to stay under cover. The division took advantage of this quiet period to make internal shifts among units. Tank companies were assigned to operate where needed on the front. Small unit headquarters were moved up closer to the front. Units on the line were rotated to give the men a rest.

On the evening of 18 January, the three-day quiet period ended, and the coastal sector was subjected to a two-hour enemy artillery barrage during which 386 rounds were reported. By the next day, the 370th Infantry was well along in its rehabilitation program and had begun training. On the front line, patrols that probed the Cinquale Canal were repulsed by accurate enemy machine gun and mortar fire. Although no contact with the enemy was made by the 371st patrols to Mount Strettoia and Seravezza, the regiment was cheered by three Polish deserters who told their L Company captors that Allied 57-mm fire had destroyed an enemy mortar observation point at Cerreta. The regiment was further elated when a fire and an explosion occurred in the enemy area near Strinato, 600 yards northeast of Mount Strettoia.

The 20th and 21st were quiet. The enemy continued to be alert but passive, so that patrols had great difficulty in their efforts to capture prisoners. Patrols pushed north toward Porta, Mount Strettoia, Mount Altissimo, Trassilico, and Gallicano. In the meantime, the Division artillery laid down massed interdictory and harassing fire on road and avenues of approach in order to prevent an enemy surprise attack. The central coast area between Highway 1 and Seravezza was considered the most favorable avenue of approach, so it received most of the attention. Highway 1 also was covered carefully by fire for 1,500 yards north of the Cinquale Canal.

On 20 January, a patrol from the 365th Infantry found evidence that the road that paralleled the eastern bank of the Serchio River had been freshly mined approximately 2,500 yards north of Gallicano. On the same day, the 371st Infantry patrols found the enemy very alert. A patrol from I Company that searched the buildings in Pian di Lago became the target of enemy machine guns that were located on the high ground to the east. Mortar fire was directed at the enemy guns, and the patrol escaped with only one casualty. At the same time, E Company attacked and killed two Germans who were guarding a house on the western slope of Mount Cauala. The occupants of the house retaliated with a heavy volume of well-aimed machine gun and small arms fire that forced the patrol to withdraw. On the coast, a patrol from A Company that tried to cross the Cinquale Canal was met by enemy machine guns and mortars. Five men were hit and two were missing when the action ended.

During the night of 22 January, there was a marked increase in enemy activity. An enemy patrol which blundered into the area held by C Company, 366th Infantry, was driven off by small arms fire. Machine pistol and machine gun fire pinned down a patrol of F Company, 366th Infantry, between Trassilico and Calomini. One officer and two enlisted men were wounded before the enemy was silenced by artillery fire and the patrol was able to withdraw. In the 371st sector, both sides were active. An 11-man enemy party observed at Pian di Lago and Mount Carchia was hit by artillery. In return, the enemy bombarded the regiment with mortar shells, wounding two H Company enlisted men. A patrol from E Company clashed with an enemy group in a cluster of houses on the western slope of Mount Cauala, and drove them out. Infantry weapons in the coastal sector fired six special concentrations at specific targets, and, in the cold, clear air, dive bombers penetrated enemy territory and bombed and strafed a rest center southwest of Carrara. Three large smoke columns attested to the accuracy of the fire as the airmen returned to their bases.

Naval gunfire support came to units located along the coast on 6 January, when two destroyers, the British HMS *Lookout* and the American USS *Woolsey*, steamed close to the Italian shore and fired at ground targets with their 5-inch guns. The HMS *Lookout* fixed on two buildings in northwestern Marina di Massa that were suspected of housing enemy command posts. Later she fired on a troublesome German battery located some 4,500 yards northeast of Marina di Massa on the high ground near Turano. The USS *Woolsey*'s guns fired on a suspected German command post in a cluster of houses near Via Guerra, approximately 200 yards inland and 500 yards from Fiume la Foce.

Routine patrols found the enemy alert as usual on 23 January. Four air forays were flown and strikes were made at a command post, a gun emplacement, a mixed motor and animal drawn supply column, and a ship in La Spezia harbor. Aside from approximately 195 rounds of harassing artillery fire that fell in the coastal sector during the afternoon of 25 January, the period from 25 to 27 January was relatively quiet. Patrols were aggressive and pushed northward to Molazzana, Vergemoli, Termini, Gallicano, and Porta, where they found the enemy alert and prepared to fight them off.

Shortly before midnight on 27 January, the enemy opened an artillery barrage, and by daylight, over 300 rounds had been dropped into the coastal sector. The weather was cold and clear the next day, and front-line regiments stepped up the frequency of their patrolling to three per battalion. Deep penetrations were made to guarantee contact.

Among the 32 prisoners that arrived at the Division POW enclosure on 28 January were 28 men from the Italia Division who said that the 1 Bersaglieri Regiment had placed only one battalion on the line in their sector at Castelnuovo di Garfagnan, and that the other two battalions would be committed only after they completed anti-partisan missions.

Throughout January, the Division continued the Infantry weapon "shoots" it had begun in December. 10th Army Group, Royal Artillery (AGRA), with two medium artillery regiments, came under operational control of the division at 1800 on 29 January, raising the combined British-American strength of the division to 1,170 officers, 58 warrant officers, and 21,338 enlisted men. During the month of January 1945, the 92nd Division captured 166 prisoners of war and sustained a total of 235 casualties, killed, wounded, and missing in action.

THE FEBRUARY OFFENSIVE

Prior to February 1945, all of the offensive efforts of the 92nd Division had been on a piecemeal basis. General Almond was anxious to launch a coordinated division attack. Pursuant to his directive, the division staff prepared a limited objective plan, under the code name FOURTH TERM, to improve positions and keep the enemy from further withdrawal of forces for their western front. The plan envisioned a three-pronged operation in the coastal sector to be preceded by diversion operations in the Serchio Valley. There were to be two phases: phase one was the seizure of the Magra Canal-Montignoso-Mount Folgorito; phase two was the capture of Massa and the Frigido River line.

The plan was based on the assumption that the 3rd Battalion, 370th Infantry, then attached to the 6th South African Armored Division, would be returned to the 92nd Division at least 72 hours prior to the time of the attack. All troops in the Serchio River Valley would be under the operational control of Brig. Gen. John E. Wood, the Assistant Division Commander.

The main effort of the Division was to be made in the center of the coastal sector by the 370th Infantry from its reserve position. The regiment was to attack in a column of battalions, passing through the left flank of the 371st Infantry and pushing over the Strettoia hills. These hills dominated Highway 1 and the coastal plain. One battalion of the 370th Infantry, as Division Reserve, would be committed on Division order. The 371st Infantry, on its right, was to push out into the rugged terrain of Mount Folgorito.

Task Force 1 was formed to take over control of the extreme left of the division. Under the command of Lt. Col. Edward L. Rowney,[5] 317th Engineer Battalion Commander, with Capt. Gilbert S. Holbrook, from the Division G-3 section as his Executive Officer, it consisted of the 3rd Battalion, 366th Infantry; C Company, 760th Tank Battalion; C Company, 317th Engineer Battalion; the 1125th Armored Field Artillery Battalion; 1st Platoon, B

The Commanding General's directive to the G-3 (his operations, plans, and training officer) to prepare a new plan each day, for his consideration, resulted in a constant search for new ideas.

Company, 701st Tank Destroyer Battalion; and 1st Platoon, A Company, 84th Chemical Mortar Battalion. This group was to cross the mouth of the Cinquale Canal and turn inland towards Highway 1, in a small pincer movement.

The forces in the coastal sector were to be supported by the Division Artillery (less these units in the Serchio Valley), the IV Corps Artillery, two light bombardment squadrons, two medium bombardment squadrons, and one heavy bombardment squadron of the Army Air Corps, plus naval support of at least one battleship, two cruisers, and three destroyers. The Division attack was to be preceded by a diversionary effort in the Serchio Valley. The 366th Infantry (less 3rd Battalion) was to improve its positions by clearing Lama di Sotto Ridge. The 365th Infantry was to clear the high ground on the east side of the Serchio River and drive the enemy from Castelnuovo.

At this time, the Division was under the command of Maj. Gen. Willis D. Crittenberger, IV Corps Commander. The plan of attack of the 92nd Division was submitted to him for approval on 15 January. On 3 February, General

Crittenberger advised General Almond that his plan, limited to the first phase only, had been approved and that the attack would be launched in compliance with the directive of Lt. Gen. Lucian K. Truscott, Jr., Fifth Army Commander, that IV Corps launch limited objective attacks in the 92nd Division sector.

For the diversionary attack in the Serchio River Valley, the 366th Infantry (less 3rd Battalion) was assigned an attack zone on the left, or west, side of the river. The 2nd Battalion was on the left, and the 1st Battalion was on the right. The 365th Infantry was assigned an attack zone on the right, or east, side of the river. The 2nd Battalion was on the left, the 1st Battalion was on the right, and the 3rd Battalion was in Regimental Reserve. The attack was launched on 4 February after several days of preliminary patrol activity. C Company, 366th Infantry, moved out against little enemy resistance, occupied Gallicano in strength, and pushed patrols further to the north. The 2nd Battalion, 366th Infantry, occupied Castelvecchio and Albiano at the base of the 3,000 foot Lama di Sotto ridge. However, the effort of a 20-man patrol to push further up the ridge to the village of Lama met enemy small arms, machine gun, and mortar fire, and the patrol returned to its own line. These advances restored the positions which had been lost in the German December attack.

The following day, 5 February, the main effort in the Serchio River Valley sector began. The 366th Infantry advanced half a mile against scattered resistance and numerous mine fields, occupied Calomini, and opened the road running west from Gallicano to Vergemoli. Attacks against Mount Faeto, a 1,500-foot peak, were strongly resisted. As Capt. Flemming W. Mathews, leading A Company, worked his way around a rocky knoll, he physically bumped into a German officer approaching from the other direction. The German officer turned and said in good English, "If either of us do anything foolish someone will get hurt." Both officers turned around and moved off in opposite directions. B Company twice advanced nearly to the top, only to be driven back by small arms and mortar fire each time. However, objectives were reached along other sections of the regimental line. On 6, 7 and 8 February, slight gains were made up the side of the mountain, and no counterattacks in any great strength were received.

On the east of the Serchio on 5 February, the 3rd Battalion, 365th Infantry, moved out against the Lama di Sotto ridge. The enemy was surprised and initial objectives were reached quickly. Some elements of the Fascist Italian Division, interspersed with the German troops of the 148th Grenadier Division, gave way. I Company occupied the village of Lama at 0710, and by 0750, L Company had passed through Sommocolonia and seized the high ground on the ridge southwest of Lama. K Company reached the ridge northeast of Lama at Mount della Stella, and all three units dug in to occupy the positions.

The 1st Battalion, 365th Infantry, moved forward to protect the left flank of the 3rd Battalion, and the 2nd Battalion, 366th Infantry, having moved from

German prisoners are brought down from the hills in the coastal sector — a scene reminiscent of one of Bill Mauldin's famous Willie & Joe cartoons from the war days.

the west side of the Serchio and been attached to the 365th Infantry, moved forward between the 1st and 2nd Battalions, 365th Infantry. The 2nd Battalion, 365th Infantry, attacked on 5 February with Capt. Bernard Yolles' F Company on the left and Capt. Robert N. Hough's G Company on the right. The battalion advanced about halfway up the Lama di Sotto ridge against stubborn resistance until late in the afternoon, when Captain Yolles was killed. His death so adversely influenced the effectiveness of his company that Lt. Colonel Schwarz, Battalion Commander, directed that E Company, commanded by Capt. William S. M. Banks, Jr., replace F Company in the assault on the morning of 6 February. Captain Banks led several small attacks, and by the end of the day, his company had gained ground abreast of G Company. Despite greatly increased artillery and mortar fire, objectives were reached, and the lines were consolidated with those of the 3rd Battalion. The 3rd Battalion repulsed several small counterattacks directed at Mount della Stella. By the end of the third day of heavy fighting, many of the enemy were killed and the battalion had suffered about 80 casualties.

The 1st Battalion, 365th Infantry, relieved the 3rd Battalion, 365th Infantry, during the night of 7-8 February but had hardly gotten into position when the 2nd Battalion, 286th Grenadier Regiment, began a series of fierce counterattacks to regain the ridge. The first, launched before daylight, in company strength, was successfully beaten off by artillery fire. Two other enemy attacks during the day were turned back also. But in the early evening of 8 February, the Germans struck with the entire battalion and swept through Lama, striking the Mount della Stella salient from three sides, forcing B and C Companies, 365th Infantry, back about 500 yards. Counterattacks continued on 9 February without additional success.

At 0630 on 10 February, the 365th Infantry attacked to regain the ridge, committing three battalion, the 3rd on the right, the 2nd in the center, and the attached 2nd Battalion, 366th Infantry, on the left. Heavy machine gun fire and mortar fire barrages were laid down by the Germans, but Italians of the 1st Bersaglieri Regiment collapsed, giving up 55 prisoners and enabling our troops to get back into Lama and onto part of the ridge southwest of the village. This success proved only temporary. The Germans renewed their pressure, and before dark the enemy again infiltrated into Lama itself.

Three additional hostile attacks on 11 February were beaten off until a fourth, estimated to include 200 Germans, forced further slight withdrawals. Activities then died down in the valley with the important Lama di Sotto ridge remaining in enemy hands. However, the 365th Infantry had advanced their positions about three quarters of a mile.

For the Division's three-pronged attack in the coastal zone, D-day was announced as 8 February and H-hour as 0600. Troops moved into assembly areas beginning at dark on 7 February. The 371st Infantry moved near

Valleochia; the 370th Infantry moved near Pozzi and Querceta; Task Force 1 (TF-1) assembled along the coastal road north of Forte dei Marmi. Advanced command posts and observation posts were occupied and opened by 0200.

At 0600 on 8 February, an audience that included General Truscott, General Crittenberger, General Almond, and some members of division staff, assembled at an observation post and watched the attack begin after an intense artillery and chemical mortar preparation. To conceal the forward movements of the tanks, large volumes of smoke were intermingled with the high explosives and the fire from the infantry weapons, tank destroyers, and tactical planes of the 86th Squadron. Initial advances were made rapidly across the wide no-man's land. Except for mines, there was very little opposition at first.

On the right, the 371st Infantry attacked towards Mount Cerreta and Mount Folgorito with the 1st Battalion on the right, the 2nd Battalion on the left, and the 3rd Battalion, less K Company, in reserve. K Company protected the right flank and established a counter-reconnaissance screen in the former 3rd Battalion sector. Mount Folgorito rises over 4,500 feet and its slopes are very precipitous. For ease of identification, the sawtooth hills leading to the peak were identified as Rocky Ridge, Main, Florida, Georgia, and Ohio 1, 2 and 3. The initial objective of the 1st Battalion, 371st Infantry, was the hostile stronghold on Main. The approaches were almost straight up, but the crest was reached. However, a small determined hostile force drove the troops back.

The 2nd Battalion assaulted Rocky Ridge with Capt. William E. Cooke's G Company on the right and Capt. Winston D. Wetlaufer's E Company on the left. Capt. Edmund Essholm's F Company was in reserve. The initial objective was taken by 1000. However, G Company was strafed by U.S. aircraft resulting in a number of casualties including Captain Cooke. F Company was committed to sustain the attack and cover the reorganization of G Company. F Company took about 25 prisoners and some equipment, killing and wounding many of the enemy. Shortly after 1030, resistance increased and the advance was retarded. The Battalion reorganized and attacked again at 2 p.m. against small arms, heavy mortars and artillery. An enemy counterattack in company strength was halted by effective artillery fire.

The attack of the 371st Infantry was resumed at 0630 on 9 February. The 1st Battalion moved slowly against small arms, machine gun, and heavy mortar fire. The 2nd Battalion was retarded by mine fields, small arms fire, and the steep slope of the hill. Some regimental reserves were committed to assist the advance without much success, and the troops were forced to reorganize and consolidate their positions. The same determined resistance was met on 10 February. The 1st Battalion made slight gains but was forced to withdraw during the early evening. The 2nd Battalion took its initial objective on Rocky Ridge during the morning and disrupted an enemy counterattack with artillery. During that night, the regiment regrouped its forces and consolidated its positions, and at 0820 on 11 February, repulsed a small counterattack with artillery, mortar, and small arms fire.

Throughout the four-day operation, most of the troops performed skillfully and courageously. Struggling was minimal, and although not all objectives were taken, an advance of 800 yards was made and held against determined resistance. About four officers and 17 enlisted men were killed and about four officers and 104 enlisted men were either wounded or missing in action.

During the night of 7-8 February, the 370th Infantry assembled in the area near Pozzi and Querceta, west of Pietrasanta. At 0600 on 8 February, the regiment attacked in a column of battalions on a narrow front with Highway 1 as its left boundary. The 3rd Battalion was in the lead followed by the 2nd Battalion with the 1st Battalion in reserve, to be committed on Division order only. It was intended that the momentum built by the lead battalion could be maintained by the other two. The initial objective was the capture of the Strettoia hill mass. For ease of identification the three crests of the Strettoia hill mass were designated "X," "Y," and "Z." "X" was the closest. Its slopes were terraced and rose to a height of about 450 feet. "Y" and "Z" were approximately 600 feet high.

At 0600 on 8 February, the 3rd Battalion, 370th Infantry, crossed the line of departure, following an artillery preparation by the 598th Field Artillery Battalion. L Company was on the left and K Company on the right. The battalion pushed through the mine fields and wire entanglements in the flat ground leading to the hill mass without encountering hostile opposition. However, as L Company made its way towards the top of "X," its advance was slowed by small arms and machine gun fire. K Company, on its right and slightly behind, also encountered heavy small arms and automatic weapons fire. L Company began to dig in. Subsequent efforts to continue the attack resulted in no progress. An artillery preparation was ordered, and I Company was committed on its left and captured hill "Y" at 1405. The 2nd Battalion was moved up onto hill "X" with orders to dig in and be prepared to resume the attack in the morning. In the meantime, the 281st Grenadier Regiment was reinforced by the 285th Grenadier Regiment and, following an inferno-like heavy mortar barrage, a counterattack against I Company was launched in the late afternoon and early evening, inflicting many casualties, including killing the company commander and wounding two other officers. In the confusion that followed, in the evacuation of hill "Y," some withdrew to hill "X" and others scattered to the rear. The 2nd Battalion on "X" came under the same mortar barrage and were pinned down by machine gun fire.

All of the 3rd Battalion troops remaining on hill "X" were attached to the 2nd Battalion. However, by 2140 all of the effectives remaining on "X" amounted to about 80 men. Most of the officers were engaged in rounding up

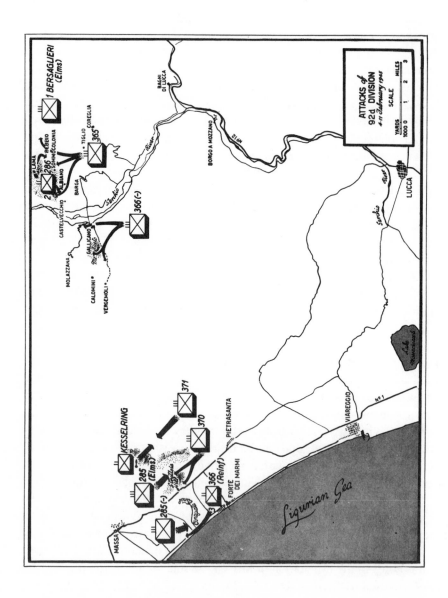

stragglers, most of whom were placed under the command of Capt. Phillip Thayer, G Company Commander. K Company, on the eastern slope of hill "X," remained intact.

Most of 9 February was spent in rounding up stragglers, reorganizing, regrouping, and consolidating. Lt. Col. Ernest V. Murphy, 2nd Battalion Commander, herded together what men he could to establish a defensive position on hill "X." I Company was unable to move forward in an effort to capture hill "Y." The 3rd Battalion assembled, in reserve, in the vicinity of Querceta. Major Curtis' 760th Tank Battalion, with A Company, 317th Engineer Battalion (less 1 platoon), 370th Anti-Tank Mine Platoon, a platoon of 370th "Raiders," and A Company, 758th Light Tank Battalion, attempted to drive up Highway 1. However, their advance was stopped when small arms and machine gun fire prevented the Engineer Battalion from removing the mine fields, and one tank was knocked out by mines.

At the close of the day General Crittenberger, IV Corps Commander, insisted that the attack be terminated. However, General Almond was adamant that it should continue for at least one more day. General Almond advised the Corps Commander that, "The Division will resume the attack tomorrow unless there is a new division commander here before that time." He insisted that his main effort, the 370th Infantry, had not had an adequate opportunity to prove itself. Further, the Division reserve had not been committed.

The 3rd Battalion, 370th Infantry, was to move to hill "X" during the night and attack at dawn to capture hill "Y." The attack began at 0630 on 10 February; however, the 3rd Battalion was halted almost before it began. Enemy mortar and artillery fire disrupted the formations to the extent that straggler lines had to be set up by the battalion commander and his staff. General Almond then directed that 371st Regimental Reserve be employed by the 370th Infantry to capture hill "Y." The 3rd Battalion, 371st Infantry, moved through the 2nd Battalion, 370th Infantry, and established a foothold on "Y" by mid-morning. The troops held their ground in a fire fight at the objective. At noon Lt. Col. Arthur H. Walker was killed and Maj. John B. Hazel assumed command of the battalion. A subsequent counterattack was repulsed. I Company, 370th Infantry, was driven from its position. After reorganization, it was returned to its position on hill "Z." The remnants of the 3rd Battalion, 370th Infantry, consisting of two officers and 80 enlisted men, were used to reinforce the troops on hill "Y" and to protect the left flank of the 3rd Battalion, 371st Infantry. The Anti-Tank Company of the 371st Infantry was moved to "Y" to relieve the 2nd Battalion, 370th Infantry (less E Company). The 2nd Battalion, 370th Infantry (less E Company), moved back to its assembly area. The officers of the 370th Infantry spent a busy night searching every house and other places for stragglers.

At 0730 on 11 February, the 281st Grenadier Regiment launched a counter-

The 3rd Battalion, 366th Infantry, on tanks moves through Forte dei Marmi followed by a ubiquitous jeep.

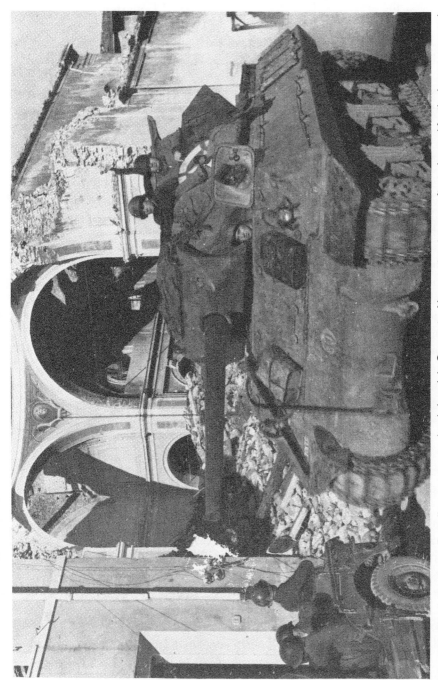

The 701st Tank Destroyer Battalion passes a ruined church in Querceta. Narrow streets were often a hazard for the larger armored vehicles.

attack against L Company, 371st Infantry, on hill "Y." As a result L Company evacuated the area in a disorderly manner. When I Company on hill "Z" discovered that its left flank was exposed by the withdrawal of L Company, it moved to the rear even though it had not been attacked. The 2nd Battalion, 370th Infantry, was directed to establish a defensive on the flat ground along the original line of departure. Determined enemy resistance, supported by heavy, effective machine gun, mortar, and artillery fire, had severely bruised and disorganized the 370th Infantry. At the end of the four-day operation, the Regiment was back on its original line of departure.

Extensive preparations were made for the divisionary envelopment by Lt. Col. Edward L. Rowney's Task Force 1 (TF 1) on the coast. For some time in the past, the headwaters of the LaFoce Canal, which empties into the Lagurian Sea at Cinquale (commonly called the Cinquale Canal), had been dammed. This resulted in the build-up of a sandbar across the mouth of the canal. The canal at its mouth was about 20 feet deep and 90 feet wide. However, the sand bar was about 30 inches deep.

The Task Force consisted of a small command group: 3rd Battalion, 366th Infantry; C Company, 760th Tank Battalion; C Company, 317th Engineer Battalion; 1st Platoon, B Company, 701st Tank Destroyer Battalion; and 1st Platoon and A Company, 84th Chemical Mortar Battalion. Capt. Gilbert S. Holbrook of the Division G-3 section assisted Lt. Colonel Rowney in his command.

The plan of maneuver called for engineers to ride across the Cinquale Canal on the lead tank of the 760th Tank Battalion, followed by infantry riding on succeeding tanks. The engineers were to dismount immediately and clear the way through the mine field for the tanks to turn inward across the beach. The infantry would dismount and under the support of tank fire, protect the engineers while they removed the mines. After the mines were cleared, the tanks, supported by infantry, were to lead the attack toward Highway 1. The tank destroyers were to be deployed immediately south of the canal to render flank supporting fire.

On the night of 4 February, the Task Force was assembled on the coast south of Viareggio. A dummy canal was marked off on the ground next to the sea and all distances were laid off on a one-to-one scale. The training was intense. Everyone was briefed and rehearsed. Officers were flown over the actual area in the Division light aircraft. The area was divided into checkerboards and each sub-area numbered so personnel could identify positions and call for supporting artillery. Telephones were added to tanks so that they could be used by infantrymen to communicate with personnel in the tanks. On the night of 7 February, the Task Force moved into position in the vicinity of Forte dei Marmi.

Lt. Colonel Rowney, Task Force 1 Commander, described the action of his

The 3rd Battalion, 366th Infantry, and 760th Tank Battalion move through Forte dei Marmi. Note how the infantry are well strung out in case of hostile fire as also are the Stuart light tanks. Everyone is in full gear with winter clothing, 8 February 1945.

command as follows:

> By 0430 I was at the starting point for the attack. I made a last minute check on all arrangements and gave the artillery the go ahead signal to begin their preparatory fire. Covered by the noise of the artillery barrage the tanks began to turn over their motors. A few minutes before the lead tank was to move out, the smoke generators began to belch their heavy white clouds, and smoke hugged the ground as though painted into the landscape. Promptly at 0500 the first wave shoved off. [Toward the river the attack started at 0600.] My command group, totaling ten persons including myself, was to follow this first Wave. The remaining two companies were to follow me. In about ten minutes the first company had cleared past me. The job of clearing mines in the gap to the sea had been done well and as far as I could see, no trouble had been encountered almost up to the mouth of the canal.

The mine field was extensive and thick, with one layer just below the surface and a second layer about three feet below the surface with a baseball-type stick on top of it. Anti-personnel mines were also scattered through the anti-tank mine field.

> I did hear some scattered machine gun fire . . . then, as I approached the mouth of the canal, the picture was changed. One of the tanks had hit a mine on the delta in the canal mouth; and another tank, the last one in line, while trying to go around it had gone into the deep water and drowned its motor. All of the other tanks had gone forward. I was pleased to find that the tank crews of both the disabled tanks stayed with their tanks and continued to fire down the canal covering the movement of troops across the canal. As far as I could tell, there had not been a single casualty up to this point.
>
> While I was comforting myself with this thought, the first of several long-range shells from the Punta Bianca naval guns near La Spezia began to land right in the mouth of the canal. The first one hit squarely in the middle of my little command group and when I looked around there were only two others who had not been hit. The shell had killed seven. The entire mouth of the canal appeared to turn red with blood.
>
> Further forward I found the next tank in line about a hundred yards ahead of the mouth of the canal. The men who had mounted it were digging in under the near side of the tank. Looking ahead I saw this same condition repeated all along the beach: the infantry dismounted and digging under the tanks. The tanks had kept a dispersed formation and cut off their motors. I ran as fast as I could in the soft sand to the head of

The attack of the 92nd Division towards La Spezia, supported by IV Corps Artillery and Engineers, was launched at 0500 on 8 February 1945. Not bad going for tanks across a sandy bottom, but rough for infantry when required to get wet like this in cold weather.

the column. There I found that two of the tanks had turned off, one about 25 yards in from the beach and the other about 15 yards in. The enemy had apparently brought small arms fire on the point of break-through and I noticed a half dozen engineer soldiers lying dead or wounded at this point. Artillery and mortar fire were falling on the tanks and it was obvious that their exposed position on the beach was the worst possible place that they could be. When I reached the lead tank I found that it had hit a mine and could go no further. I gathered together a handful of engineers and had them prod for mines with bayonets. Then I instructed the commander of the second tank to try to pass the first tank. It worked. We now had one disabled tank about 25 yards in from the beach and a good one about 60 yards from the beach.

I got behind the first of the tanks along the beach and told the men to move forward to join the lead tanks. They did not move but kept digging further and further into their holes behind the tanks. At this point I saw the sergeant from the first tank that had hit a mine. He suggested that if we could clear some of the dead and wounded away from the cleared lane in from the beach, that perhaps the troops would be more inclined to move forward. During the next half hour we removed ten dead to a clump of trees out of view; and about 20 of the wounded were taken to the basement of a bombed-out house. . . .

When this was completed, Colonel Rowney and the tank sergeant escorted little groups forward toward the most forward tanks.

Then I'd get a group of six to ten behind the third tank, the forward one on the beach, and we'd bound off together up towards the first two tanks. Running or even trying to walk in the loose white sand of the beach was tiring and my legs soon became leaden. I went back to the tail of the column for a breather and let the sergeant push a group up behind the number three tank. I had been counting my trips up and back but after the seventh trip I lost count.

By noon the first wave was completely off the beach and was somewhere in the vicinity of the first two tanks.

I Company followed M Company across the Cinquale Canal and by 1030 was beyond the coastal road. K Company was the last of the 3rd Battalion, 366th Infantry, to cross the canal. By noon they too were just beyond the coastal road. There were many stragglers and many men returned south across the Cinquale.

While this was going on, Major Willis D. Polk, the battalion commander, came toward me. I noticed that he had been shot in the shoulder. He told me that he wanted to reassure me that he was up forward doing everything that he could to get the men into position and that he would have to be hit harder than he was to make him stop. There was no bravado in his voice — it was filled with sincerity. Later that afternoon I found him lying in the vicinity of the lead tank with a bullet hole between his eyes.

While organizing the defensive position in the east-west line, I could hear the sound of German burpguns building up off to the left flank. An enemy counterattack of perhaps platoon strength was coming straight south down the beach. Several of the tank commanders had huddled together and were debating what to do about it. They seemed to agree on a solution collectively which no individual would want to dispute: to stay where they were and repel the counterattack. Returning from the beach I found Lieutenant Johnson, the engineer platoon commander, who with a force of twenty or twenty-five men moved to a knob of the high ground on the left front overlooking the beach. His mission was to fire in the general direction of the sea and to be prepared to repel the counterattack should it come further down the beach. The tank commander called for artillery using his grid system and the artillery came down promptly right in front of the advancing enemy. Continued artillery fire and machine gun strafing from the tank, plus the fire which was coming from the platoon, broke up the counterattack.

I was elated. We had stood off an attack. However, it was only a small one. What if the enemy put a larger force against us — say a company? I became apprehensive over the small volume of fire that had come from the platoon, and asked the men about it. Their answer was that the rifles were full of sand and would not fire. All along the line instructions were issued to clean rifles. The precaution of seeing that oil and thongs were in the cleaning compartment of the rifle had paid off.

Shortly after noon, Lt. Colonel Arnold, Division G-3, made a personal reconnaissance of the leading elements north of the Cinquale Canal. There amid continuous hostile small arms fire and with our troops deployed at his feet, he conferred with Lt. Colonel Rowney. At that time he learned that the 3rd Battalion, 366th Infantry, had sustained heavy casualties and that the Battalion Commander, Executive Officer, and S-3 had been killed. Further, he discovered that the senior company commander, with no battalion level experience, was in command of the battalion. After spending the afternoon observing the operations and assisting in returning stragglers into battle, Lt. Colonel Arnold concluded that if the initial success of establishing a beach-head north of the Cinquale Canal was to be exploited, reinforcements would be required. Based on his recommendation, B Company, 370th Infantry, was attached to the 3rd Battalion, 366th Infantry, and arrived in the area north of the Cinquale Canal about 1700. Lt. Colonel Arnold led the Company Commander into the area and pointed out to him the situation on the ground. The Company Commander decided to use the ditch on the west side of the coastal road as a line of departure. B Company was deployed on this line. As the Company Commander was about to give the order to move out, an artillery barrage from the big coastal guns at Punta Bianca in the La Spezia area fell up and down the ditch, on B Company. Evacuation of casualties and reorganization caused the company to delay its forward movement.

I issued instructions to the tank commander to get more of his tanks off the beach and into the east-west line. However, I did not spend much time with the tanks, as I felt that organizing the infantry position before dark was more important. Several of the tanks managed to come into the line and by dusk six or seven of the tanks were deployed along the beach-half of the defense line.

In the lull before dark, I was able to talk to most of the officers and formulate plans for the night. We had feeble radio communication with the rear. The radio had gone completely dead. Both telephone lines had been repeatedly blased out by the artillery which was still landing all along the beach. I knew that it was useless to count on it being repaired.

As night came on I had a short-lived feeling of confidence. The unit had reached its position and had stayed all day. That was something. And while the small arms fire was light, that area had taken the greatest concentration of enemy artillery fire I had ever seen. [Later I learned from information furnished us by Fifth Army Headquarters that this area received the greatest single concentration of artillery fire of the entire Italian Campaign. Looking back on it now I can well believe it. There did not seem to be a single patch of ground anywhere that was not covered with artillery fragments.]

About 150 men, all that was left of the battalion, were dug in to what seemed to be a tenable defense line. Several of the soldiers digging in struck mines. This added to the number of wounded and further demoralized the already badly depressed men.

The main line was about 100 yards forward in the east-west road. In the center and on the south side of this road I had established my command post in a small one-story concrete building. Fifty soldiers, under Lieutenant Johnson, dug in at the rear of the Command Post, where I could reach them if I needed a reserve.

Darkness fell about 2030. Shortly before 2200 a steady increase in the sound of burp guns came from the east down the east-west road. Flares began to drop in the area, bathing the road and buildings in light. The tank farthest to the east was instructed to fire to the east. A half dozen men were placed about a hundred yards forward of the tank in order to make sure that no Germans would attack the tanks with bazookas. The sound of the burp guns came closer and closer and then the fire from the tank stopped. There seemed to be very little fire coming from our side. The suspense became unbearable. I issued instructions to the tiny reserve near my Command Post to deploy across the east-west road. After some confused exchange of shots, quite a few of them ricocheting off the building, the enemy fire stopped. The Germans could have taken the Command Post but for some unknown reason they backed off.

A few minutes before midnight another counterattack of the same type occurred. Again there was some confusion and this time the enemy came down the road and passed the Command Post. And again, after an exchange of fire they withdrew.

We were sure that at 0200 the performance would be repeated. The minutes seemed to drag on. "Would it never get light?" The tension mounted and praying and moaning became audible. Another counterattack came down the east-west road promptly on schedule, at 0200. This time the Germans must have gone all the way to the beach. We could hear them talking and shouting. Several voices came close to the building, there was an exchange of fire, several grenades went off against the side of the building, and again they moved away. The next morning we found two Germans dead in the doorways of the Command Post.

There were no signs of any more Germans and contrary to our expectations, there was no attack at 0400. As dawn broke I began to look around to see what there was left. Only a handful of men were in their defensive positions. Several had been wounded and others had remained. The others had drifted to the rear.

Communications between 92nd Division Headquarters and Task Force 1 was very poor. Occasionally it was possible to get messages through by radio from the Artillery Forward Observer to his 1125th Field Artillery Battalion Headquarters, to 92nd Division Artillery Headquarters, and to the 92nd Division Headquarters, and from one of the medium tanks to its 760th Battalion Headquarters and to Division Headquarters. Headquarters 92nd Division was unable to reach either Task Force 1 or 3rd Battalion, 366th Infantry Headquarters by radio, and the 92nd Division Signal Company was unable to establish wire communications.

Captain Holbrook returned to 92nd Division Headquarters about 1800 on 8 February, with a situation report. He was ordered to return to Task Force 1 Headquarters about 2100 to deliver a copy of Operation Instructions No. 2,

A foot injured by an anti-personnel mine, the black soldier on the right bites his tongue as he hobbles to the rear, already on morphine.

directing completion of one Infantry support raft and two foot bridges and resumption of the attack at 0630 on 9 February. Captain Holbrook was mortally wounded en route.

The task force positions and their approaches were under heavy fire from both sides throughout the night. The artillery and mortar shelling delayed the building of bridges, and interfered with the movement of supplies to the troops on the north bank. Enemy machine guns that played up and down the canal disrupted work details and generally slowed the support for the attack. By the middle of the afternoon of 9 February, about 60 men were dug in on the defense line along the Montignoso Road.

About mid-morning on 9 February, Lt. Colonel Arnold again visited the area of Task Force 1. He met Maj. Richard G. Tindall, 92nd Division Signal Officer, at the Cinquale Canal and offered his assistance in establishing a wire link with the engaged forces. The offer was declined. One-half hour later Major Tindall was killed.

In view of the excessive straggling of the 3rd Battalion, 366th Infantry, the high casualties that had left some companies with only a handful of men, and the apparent lack of command and control, Lt. Colonel Arnold concluded that another battalion headquarters and headquarters company would be required. Lt. Col. Harold R. Everman, Commanding Officer, 1st Battalion, 370th Infantry, moved his battalion headquarters and headqurters company into the sector to take over command of Task Force 1. Lt. Colonel Rowney returned to Division Headquarters. The 758th Light Tank Battalion was attached and used to ferry Lt. Colonel Everman and his headquarters across the Cinquale Canal.

Continuous artillery and mortar shelling of the canal, especially at the crossing near its mouth, interrupted all supply effort. Supplies had to be carried by hand across the canal in the absence of a bridge. Tanks were finally pressed into service as supply vehicles and the situation improved under this arrangement. North of the canal, the heavy mine fields restricted the movement of tanks, and it was almost impossible to keep the wire circuits in order. Mines were placed at such depths that even after it was believed that a path was clear and a number of tanks had passed over it, a mine would explode and disable another tank.

Shortly before dark, Lt. Colonel Everman had his A Company in position, and he took command of the remnants of the original force, with the 3rd Battalion, 366th Infantry, staying as an attachment. Heavy machine gun fire, and mortar and artillery fire, hit Lt. Colonel Everman's troops on 10 February. A counterattack at 0600 forced A Company into a limited withdrawal, but supporting artillery and tanks repulsed this threat. Another counterattack at 1100 was also turned back; but a third one at 1730 drove the entire force back 200 to 500 yards. C Company was rushed up by truck from division reserve to be ready to move into battle, if needed.

Critique after Battle. Lt. Colonel Arnold reviews the successes and failures of the February attack with the 3rd Battalion, 366th Infantry.

However, it was now apparent that further attempts to advance would be futile. Straggling was excessive and disorganization was evident in nearly every unit across the division front of the coastal zone. General Almond ordered a termination of the attack. The 370th and 371st Infantry Regiments were ordered to consolidate their positions and to reconstitute their reserves. Lt. Colonel Everman was ordered to withdraw his Task Force to the south side of the canal and to organize positions there. This action was covered by tanks and was completed by 0400 on 11 February. L Company, 366th Infantry, remained as an attachment of 1st Battalion, 370th Infantry, and moved into the old defensive positions occupied before the attack. The 1st Battalion, 370th, assembled in the vicinity of Forte dei Marmi. The 3rd Battalion, 366th, also assembled in that vicinity and then moved to a rehabilitation area south of Viareggio for regrouping and training. That night the 92nd Military Police Platoon was ordered to patrol the coastal sector until the 1st Battalion, 370th Infantry, could be reorganized and regrouped and effectively exercise control over the sector.

Brig. Gen. Otto Fretter-Pico, Commanding General of the 148th Grenadier Division, reacted to the 92nd Division attack in a postwar interview with Lt. Colonel Arnold as follows:

My initial reaction to the attack of the 92nd Division on 8 to 11 February 1945 was that of not too much concern as I knew that the 92nd Division had not received front line replacements for this attack. I did not consider this action as a major offense, but only as an attack to relieve the fight at the main front. I was right in that the attack was halted and no other attacks followed immediately.

The 92nd Division's limited objective attack achieved a slight improvement of positions, but the main contribution was that they had kept enemy forces pinned down in this sector and served to keep the enemy confused as to future Allied intentions. Further, a considerable amount of information as to hostile strength and disposition was developed. This proved to be of considerable value during the spring offensive. However, the four-day attack was costly for the 92nd Division. A total of 47 officers and 659 enlisted men were killed, wounded, or missing in action. One half of the casualties were sustained by the 3rd Battalion, 366th Infantry, whose casualties totaled 329, approximately one half of their total strength. Lost were 24 tanks and many other pieces of equipment.

On 23 February the 92nd Division sector was extended to the 44 Easton. At that time, the 473rd Infantry Regiment (white), made up of converted anti-aircraft troops, came under Division control. The next day, General Almond issued Field Order No. 9 announcing that the Division would hold the

INFANTRY -TANK TEAM

Team work between infantry and tanks was constantly stressed and practiced.

maximum enemy force in the coastal sector and exert pressure within its capabilities. the 473rd Infantry relieved the 366th Infantry and assumed control of the Serchio Valley section. The 366th Infantry moved to the Division Training Area south of Viareggio and began a rehabilitation and training program. On 28 February, the 365th Infantry was relieved from the 92nd Division and assumed command of the Cutigliana Sector under IV Corps control. During the month of February, the 92nd Division's casualties totaled 62 officers and 1,191 enlisted men killed, wounded, or missing in action. The Division captured 1,001 prisoners of war.

REGROUPING, REORGANIZATION AND PLANS FOR SPRING OFFENSIVE

About the same time the 92nd Division was conducting its February offensive, the 1st Canadian Corps was alerted to leave Italy and join other Canadian forces on the Western Front. By mid-March, the Canadian Corps had left the 15th Army Group en route to France.

The loss of the Canadian Corps was partially compensated for by the arrival of some new units, the retaining of units already in the theater for use as infantry, and the use of Italian forces. The main body of the 10th Mountain Division arrived from the U.S. in January. The Italian Cremona Group, Legnano Group, Folgore Group, and Friuli Group, each containing two infantry regiments, one artillery regiment, and one engineer battalion, with a combat strength of about two-thirds the size of an American division, became available at intervals throughout the winter. They were organized similar to Eighth Army's Jewish Infantry Brigade. However, the Jewish Brigade had three infantry regiments, one artillery regiment, and one engineer company. Nearly a dozen new artillery battalions, some from Yugoslavia, which had been supporting Mahalavitch, were also received. The Japanese-American 442nd Infantry was scheduled to return to Italy from France.

In January 1945, Headquarters 2nd Armored Group, the 434th, 435th, 532nd and 900th Anti-Aircraft Artillery Automatic Weapons Battalions were moved to Montecatini, Italy, and reorganized as the 473rd Infantry Regiment. Col. Willis D. Cronk, who had commanded the 2nd Armored Group, assumed command of the new regiment. The 1st Battalion was commanded by Lt. Col. Peter L. Urban, the 2nd Battalion by Lt. Col. Hampton H. Lisle, and the 3rd

Maj. Gen. Alfred M. Grunther, Gen. Mark W. Clark, Gen. of the Army George C. Marshall, Lt. Gen. Lucian K. Truscott, Maj. Gen. Edward M. Almond, Lt. General McNarney, and Maj. Gen. Willis D. Crittenberger.

Gen. of the Army George C. Marshall and Maj. Gen. Edward M. Almond accompanied by Lt. Col. Thomas St. J. Arnold and a Military Police security detachment.

Chief of Staff, U.S. Army, Gen. of the Army George C. Marshall, Maj. Gen. Edward M. Almond, Col. Raymond G. Sherman, Sergeant Parks, Maj. Gen. Willis D. Crittenberger, and Lt. Col. Thomas St. J. Arnold during General Marshall's visit to the Italian campaign, 1945.

Battalion by Maj. Paul Woodward. After only 31 days of intensive infantry training, the regiment was committed in a defensive role on the night of 15 February on the right of the 92nd Division. It was attached to Task Force 45, under the Command of IV Corps. Two days later, on 17 February, Col. William P. Yarborough relieved Colonel Cronk who was assigned to Fifth Army Headquarters.

Following the 92nd Division's failure to capture Massa in early February, General Almond began to search for ways to increase the combat effectiveness of his infantry units. Further, General Clark, who continued to search for ways to make up for the loss of five divisions, was of the opinion that it was vital for the success of the capture of Bologna for Fifth Army to maintain an offensive attitude on the west coast and to be capable of capturing La Spezia. This led to a series of discussions and letters between Generals Marshall, Clark, Truscott, Crittenberger, and Almond. Finally, General Marshall proposed that the most reliable elements of the three infantry regiments of the 92nd Division be combined into one regiment and that the 473rd (white) and 442nd (Japanese-American) Infantry Regiments be attached as the other two regiments of the division.

Accordingly, over a three-week period, from 24 February to 17 March, 70 officers and 1,359 enlisted men holding decorations and/or Combat Infantry-man Badges were transferred into the 370th Infantry from the 365th and 371st Infantry, and 52 officers and 1,264 enlisted men were transferred out. The 473rd Infantry was attached to the 92nd Division on 24 February and directed to move into the Serchio River Valley. By 28 February, the regiment relieved the 365th and 366th Infantry and was conducting an active defense of its new sector.

Following its relief on 28 February, the 365th Infantry moved to the east and assumed responsibility for the Cutigliano sector under IV Corps. The 366th Infantry moved to the Division Training Area south of Viareggio. There it turned in all of its infantry equipment. On 29 March, the regiment was relieved of Division control, and moved to the vicinity of Bottinoccio. There it was converted into two general service engineer regiments, less one battalion. At that time, Fifth Army had a vital need for additional engineers. In addition to employing Italian engineers and a wide use of civilians for engineer purposes, it had converted several anti-aircraft units to engineers. On his return to the United States from the meeting of Roosevelt, Churchill, and Stalin at Yalta on the Black Sea, General Marshall visited the 92nd Division on 28 February to observe its operations and give his final approval to its reorganization. He visited Infantry, Engineer, and other combat and support-ing units.

The Bronze Star was the lowest decoration that could be awarded for valor. General Marshall believed the courage and valor displayed by every Infantry-

General Almond de-
briefs a 473rd Infantry
Regiment patrol that had
spent five days scouting
behind enemy lines.

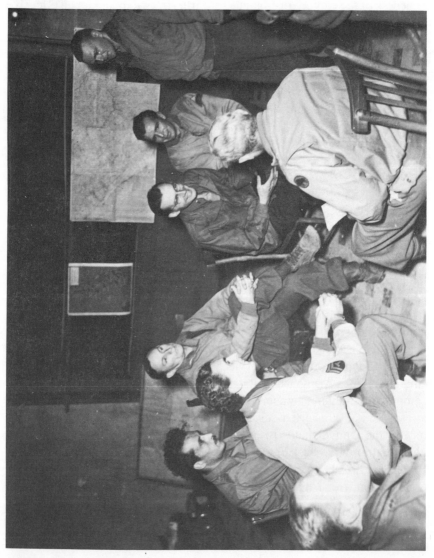

600th Field Artillery Battalion in firing position.

From Spy to Spy

During the war against Germany, operations of the Office of Strategic Services, the U. S. "cloak and dagger" agency, were so hush-hush that one section seldom knew about the work of another. For the first two years of the war there was no coordination between the division dealing with dissemination of false rumors in Axis territory and the one that gathered secret intelligence there. A check one day by a curious Army colonel in the agency disclosed that nearly half the information of the secret intelligence files actually originated from the division disseminating the false rumors.

A clipping from "YANK," an Army publication.

man who bore his breast to enemy bullets in combat should be recognized. Consequently, he devised the Combat Infantryman's Badge and guarded it carefully. When he met Lt. Colonel Rowney, 317th Engineer Combat Battalion Commander, he pointed deliberately at his chest and said in a stern manner, "Where did you get that?" Lt. Colonel Rowney said, "General Almond gave it to me." General Marshall turned to General Almond and said, "Why?!" General Almond responded, "Because I think he is a damn good Infantry-man." General Marshall did not know, at that time, that Lt. Colonel Rowney had led the 3rd Battalion, 366th Infantry, reinforced with Tanks, Artillery, and Engineers in their attack across the Cinquale Canal on 8-11 Feburary.

That night, at the Division Forward Officer's Mess, General Marshall said, "With the conduct of a global war, you would think that my chief concern would be planning for and the conduct of grand strategy, but, that is not the case. My chief concern is to prevent my friends in responsible positions from gobbling up all of the available manpower and putting them in their headquar-ters."

Although the newspapers characterized the actions of the 473rd Infantry during the month of March as conducting "routine patrol activity in the Serchio Valley," their "power" patrols were better described as small-scale limited objective attacks. On 2 March at 0600, two platoons of C Company assaulted the ridge just north of hill 437. Hostile forces were in well-prepared positions and shortly after the attack started, a number of men fell in the center of C Company's line. One of the platoons was led by Sgt. Frank J. Pustka. His platoon was pinned down by fire from a machine gun less than 100 yards away. Although wounded by a grenade, Sergeant Pustka worked his way forward and knocked out the machine gun with white phosphorus grenades.

On 5 and 6 March, Lt. Colonel Redding's 701st Tank Destroyer Battalion staged a tank demonstration to deceive the enemy as to tank strength in the Serchio Valley, as Major Curtis' 760th Tank Battalion moved to the coastal sector. On 6 March, the 679th Tank Destroyer Battalion (towed) was attached to the Division.

During March a number of successful tank-infantry type raids were conducted by the 473rd Infantry on enemy positions. One such raid was conducted early on 7 March by a platoon of Anti-Tank Company, commanded by Capt. Ben H. Nevers, attached to the 1st Battalion and supported by the 751st Tank Battalion. The force destroyed the enemy outpost at Casa Broglia, killing and capturing 24 of the 25 manning the position. Other raids by power patrols resulted in additional slight gains in the Serchio Valley.

On 17 March the reorganized 370th Infantry began an intensive training program in the Division training area. The 442nd Infantry and the 23rd Engineer Company (Japanese-American), under the command of Lt. Col. Virgil R. Miller, arrived at Leghorn after a very tiring trip from France in open

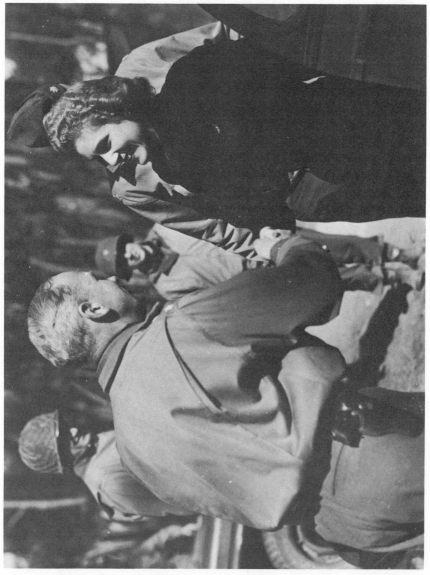

Maj. General Almond welcomes Congresswoman Clare Booth Luce, wife of the owner of *Time* and *Life*, to the 92nd Division.

landing crafts. These units were moved to a training area just north of Lucca and attached to the 92nd Division on 25 March. Here, they received the infantry equipment which had been turned in by the 366th Infantry and intensive training was conducted. Command and training inspections were conducted by General Almond and the staff of the 92nd Division.

On 25 March the 111th Army Field Regiment, Royal Artillery, was attached to the Division. The 111th Army Field Regiment, Royal Artillery, had been supporting the partisans in Yugoslavia before the Allies changed their support from Mahalavitch to Tito. General Almond was directed to prepare plans to employ the reorganized 92nd Division (370th, 442nd, and 473rd Infantry Regiments) in an attack, with limited objectives, in the coastal sector at the earliest practical date. The 370th Infantry, at least in part, was to be employed in the attack. Accordingly, the 92nd Division Plan "SECOND WIND," to seize Massa and the line of the Frigido River, was prepared.

This plan resembled Plan "FOURTH TERM" in aim, but differed from it in content. To shield the attacking troops from the heavy coastal guns at Punta Bianca, it was planned to push two regiments through the rugged peaks that overlooked the flat coastal area concurrently while having the coastal guns attacked by medium or heavy air bombardment. The main effort was to be along a line from Mount Folgorito through the western Mount Belvedere and on to the north of Mount Brugiana. By clearing these mountain ridges, it was expected that the enemy on the Mount Strettoia hill would be forced to evacuate the plain in front of Massa.

Operations during the month of March resulted in the loss of 2 officers and 41 enlisted men killed, 6 officers and 157 enlisted men wounded in action, and 2 officers and 16 enlisted men missing in action. A total of 516 prisoners of war were captured. By 1 April, the 92nd Division had completed its reorganization and was ready to launch its spring offensive. Morale was high and the troops were ready to go.

3.

Po Valley Campaign

5 April - 8 May 1945

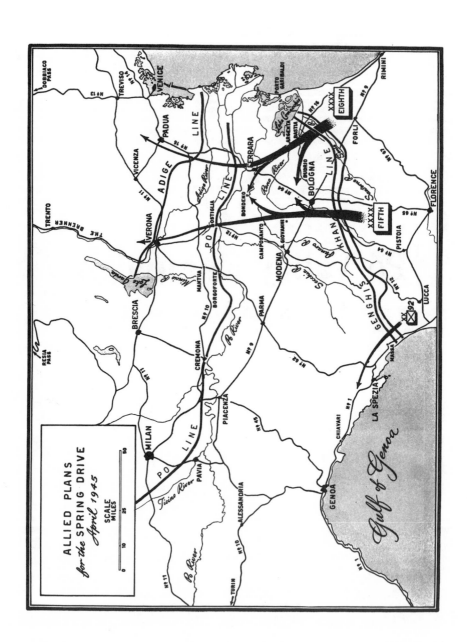

ALLIED PLANS
for the SPRING DRIVE
April 1945

SCALE
MILES
0   10   25   50

PREPARATION FOR THE SPRING OFFENSIVE

With the approach of spring, the officers and enlisted men of the Allied forces in northern Italy felt a new sense of confidence. As plans and preparations were being made for General Clark's 15th Army Group Spring Offensive, a general feeling of impending success in the defeat of German forces was developed.

During the period of January to April 1945, the German High Command withdrew four divisions from Italy to be deployed on other fronts. The remaining enemy forces in Italy totaled 24 German divisions, 5 Italian divisions in Marshal Graziani's Ligurian Army, and Prince Borghese's Borghese Division (Italian), Prince Borghese's private army. The Borghese Division was maintained in Marshal Kesselring's Army Group C reserve. Prince Borghese was a member of an Italian noble family from Siena. The title of Prince had been bestowed on his ancestors by the Pope at the time the Church was conquering territory.

The 10th Flotilla Mass, a Naval force, privately supported by Prince Borghese, operated in the Ligurian Sea off of the left flank of the 92nd Division. It operated from bases in Genoa and La Spezia. It is believed that the flotilla contained three squadrons. One consisted of paddle-foot sailors. Their mission was to swim out into the harbor at Leghorn and place explosive charges on the side of ships. Although the merchant seamen on board the ships periodically dropped hand grenades over the side to discourage such activities, they were successful in damaging a number of ships.

ENEMY DISPOSITIONS
9 APRIL 1945

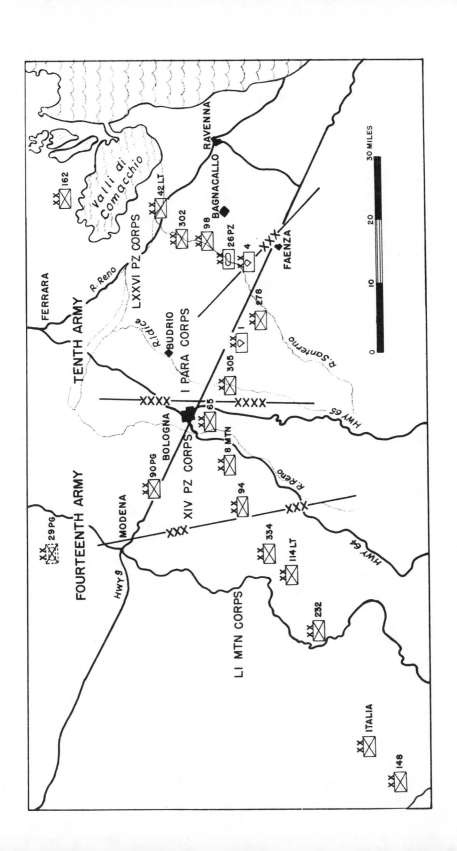

A second squadron, equipped with high-speed boats, was employed to attack ships relatively close to shore. These boats were made of plywood and carried a ton of high explosives in the bow. They were equipped with a single Alfa-Romeo motor and could travel at 55 miles per hour. The fuse was fitted into the nose of the craft. The coxswain stood on a catapult in the rear of the boat. Just before ramming a ship, he would pull a lever releasing the catapult, projecting him into the air, and he would swim away to safety.

The third squadron, equipped with slightly larger high-speed boats, was operated to attack shipping further out to sea. These boats were also made of plywood. They were equipped with two Alfa-Romeo motors, with a long well in between. A conventional torpedo was carried in this well. The crafts were capable of traveling at 35 miles per hour. When a target was sighted, the boat would approach at maximum speed, do a 180-degree turn, eject the torpedo, and speed away as fast as possible.

On entering Genoa, Lt. Colonel Arnold's 598th Field Artillery Battalion captured a number of these boats. He subsequently used them for recreational purposes off the coast of Santa Margherita and Porto Fino, based at Villa Parregi. However, before using the small crafts, it was necessary to dispose of the ton of TNT in the bows. The solution was to take the boats out to sea, cut all wires and cables with an ax, and heave the high explosives over the side. This left the boat standing on its stern until the bow was weighted with sandbags.

After the cessation of hostilities, Prince Borghese utilized his personnel to establish roadblocks and prevent Italians from traveling from one community to the next, through northern Italy. He hoped his reign of terror would inspire the people to overthrow the House of Savoy and make him king. The House of Savoy was ousted; however, a democracy was established instead.

Facing Eighth Army was the 162nd Infantry Division, the 42nd Jaeger Division, the 362nd Infantry Division, the 98th Infantry Division, the 26th Panzer Division, the 4th Parachute Division, the 278th Infantry Division, the 1st Parachute Division, and the 305th Infantry Division. Before the Fifth Army was the 65th Infantry Division, the 8th Mountain Division, the 94th Infantry Division, the 334th Infantry Division, the 114th Jaeger Division, the 232nd Infantry Division, the Italia Division, and the 148th Grenadier Division.

In local reserve, the 90th Panzer Grenadier Division, commanded by Col. Hans F. Wunderlich, was located in the vicinity of Budrio, with elements between Bologna and Modena. In more distant reserve were two German and three Italian divisions in Northwest Italy and four German divisions in Northeast Italy. There was also the German 24th SS Division and a German-officered Italian SS Division in Italy, both suitable only for internal security, but which might be used in extreme circumstances.

During the winter much assistance was given to the Italian partisans, who became stronger and more effective in sabotaging German installations and equipment and harassing the enemy's lines of communication. Many tons of supplies in the form of weapons, ammunition, food, clothing, and medical supplies were dropped by air to the partisans. Allied liaison officers, parachuted into Northern Italy, did an outstanding job of coordinating partisan activities and communicating with Allied headquarters.

In preparation for the spring offensive, the 92nd Division floated a small boat up the Ligurian coast with its sides only a few inches above the water line, with 1,500 red arm bands for partisan identification. The instructions to the partisans were, "Some time in the near future the 92nd Division will launch a coordinated attack. You will know when it happens. At that time you are to seize and prevent the destruction of all of the bridges from our leading elements to Genoa. Those guarding the bridges are to wear the red arm bands for identification."

Facing the 92nd Division, under the command of Brig. General Fretter-Pico, were the 148th Grenadier Division and the Italia Division together with two additional German battalions and five additional Italian Battalions. All of them were on commanding terrain in well-prepared fortified positions of the Gothic Line. Defending the Serchio Valley was the 268th Grenadier Regiment with the Reconnaissance Battalion, Italia Division; 1st Battalion, 1st Bersaglieri Regiment; 2nd Battalion, 2nd Bersaglieri Regiment; and 3rd Battalion, 3rd Bersaglieri Regiment attached.

Defending the coastal sector were the 281st Grenadier Regiment; 2nd Batallion, 285th Grenadier regiment; Fusilier Battalion, 148th Grenadier Division; Kesselring Machine Gun Battalion; 4th Mountain Battalion; 101st Cavalry Reconnaissance Battalion; and the Intra Alpine Battalion, Monte Rosa Division. Available as local reserves were the 285th Grenadier Regiment, less one battalion, and the possible use of sailors on duty at La Spezia. General Fretter-Pico was apprehensive of an amphibious operation on his right flank. In a postwar interview, he told Colonel Arnold that "My principal worry, prior to the April attack, was the possibility of an attack from the sea. Such an action would have made my position untenable."

General Clark's 15th Army Group plan of attack was to be executed in three phases:

I: The breaching of the Santerno River by the Eighth Army and the debouchment of the Fifth Army into the Po Valley; this phase included the capture or isolation of Bologna.

II: The breakthrough by either or both Armies to encircle the German forces south of the Po River.

III: The crossing of the Po River and the capture of Verona.

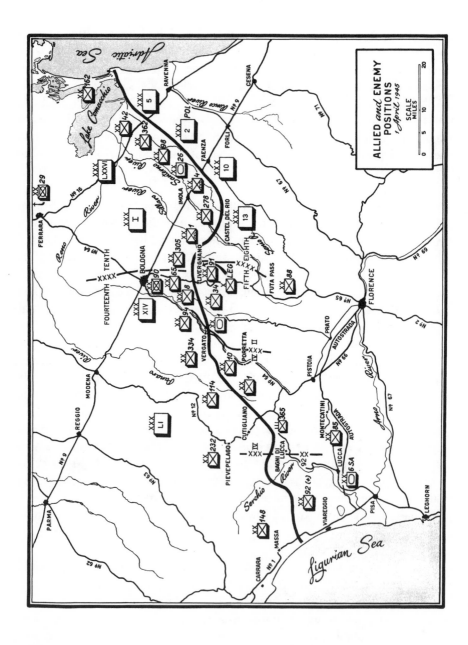

It was hoped that the operation could be executed without a pause between any of the phases. Eighth Army was to attack first, a few days before D-day, followed by the Fifth Army. This timing was to keep the enemy guessing as to Allied intentions and to permit the full weight of air support to be given to each Army in succession. Fifth Army was to make the main effort with II and IV Corps attacking along Highway 64 towards Bologna. D-day was set for 10 April (later changed to 9 April).

A diversionary attack was to be launched by the 92nd Division, in the coastal sector, to capture Massa, beginning on 5 April. This effort was expected to tie down the German 148th Grenadier Division, reinforced, in the area and prevent its use at a later time in the Bologna area. There was also the remote possibility that it might attract the 90th Panzer Grenadier Division. The 92nd Division Plan envisioned having the 370th Infantry pass through elements of the 371st Infantry and push forward through the lower hills in a column of Battalions, through Montignoso to Massa, branch off to the Ligurian Sea north of the Cinquale Canal, then turn to the north, and drive on to the Frigido River. No attempt would be made to cross the Cinquale Canal near the sea.

The 442nd Infantry was to pass through the other portion of the 371st Infantry and seize the dominating terrain around Mount Altissimo, drive towards Carrara, and then cut off the heavily-defended plains. It was to bypass Massa and seize Mount Brugiana. The 473rd Infantry (less its 2nd Battalion) was to carry out a demonstration in the Serchio Valley and conduct aggressive patrolling in order to hold the forces on its front. The 2nd Battalion, 473rd Infantry, was to be retained in Division Reserve, ready to support the attack of the 370th Infantry or the 442nd Infantry. The 371st Infantry (less its 2nd Battalion) after being passed through by the 370th and 442nd Infantries, was to remain in position and support the attack by fire until relieved from attachment to the 92nd Division and moved to the IV Corps zone.

In preparation for its attack on the left flank of 15th Army Group, the 92nd Division was reinforced by the attachment of an array of forces. Before the completion of its offensive operations, the total strength of the Division was approximately 25,000 men and officers. The 760th Medium Tank Battalion which had joined the Division in December and left it in January was again attached on 3 April. Others joining the Division in late March and early- to mid-April were the 329th Field Artillery Battalion (85th Division), the 530th Field Artillery Battalion (155-mm guns, less one battery), the 679th Tank Destroyer Battalion (towed), the British 76th Heavy Anti-Aircraft Regiment, and the 232nd Engineer Combat Company.

In addition to the Allied fighter bomber air support of leading elements, medium and heavy bomber attacks were scheduled for the coastal defense artillery, including six 152-mm guns, four 128-mm guns and a number of 90-

mm dual purpose guns on Punta Bianca near La Spezia employed by the Germans in a ground support role. The 1st Armored Division was in a reserve position, under Army control, in the vicinity of Lucca. In order to confuse the enemy and to prevent the movement of hostile reserves from the Serchio sector to the coastal sector, the 92nd Division moved a dummy armored division up the Serchio Valley from Bagni di Lucca to Barga on the nights of 3 and 4 April. This was followed by heavy artillery concentrations simulation on artillery preparation.

In a postwar interview, General Fretter-Pico stated to Colonel Arnold, "Initially, we were misled by your dummy armored division. I delayed moving reserve units from the Serchio Valley to the coastal area for two days, while waiting to see if any attack would be launched from that area. The lack of fire from high velocity weapons led us to believe that there was no appreciable concentration of armor in the area."

PRELIMINARY ATTACK

Under 15th Army Group orders, the 92nd Division was to launch a limited objective attack, as a feint, along the Ligurian Coast, with the purpose of taking Massa, five miles from its front lines, behind the strong defenses of the Gothic Line.

The terrain facing the 92nd Division consisted of a three-mile coastal plain on the west, a range of almost impassable mountains 10 to 15 miles wide in the center, and the Serchio Valley, some five miles wide on the east. Since the coastal plain was the only flat open approach to the north, the enemy had made it his most heavily defended line. Further, this area was dominated by observation from the high ground to the west. In the immediate front was the Cinquale Canal. Two miles beyond this canal the Frigido River extended across the plain. Behind that lay Carrione Creek and the Parmignola Canal before the Magra River was reached, halfway between Massa and La Spezia. If forced from his initial positions, the enemy was prepared to make a stand on each of these successive fortified water lines, generally called the Green line defenses of his Gothic Line system. From La Spezia to Genoa, the mountains extend virtually to the water's edge, offering excellent defenses by means of numerous demolitions.

Adjacent to the coastal plain lay one of the most formidable mountain ranges in Italy. While the central chain was unsuitable for any extensive military operations, the lower ranges extending toward Highway 1 and the sea offered a possibility of an advance, despite their rugged nature. Between the lower Apennines and the Serchio Valley lay the main Apennine chain, 13 miles wide at this point and extending 25 miles to the northwest with peaks as high as 6,000 feet.

On the eve of the offensive the 92nd Division held a front of 22 airline miles, extending from a point on the coast southwest of Massa to Seravezza, then north to Mount Cauala and Azzano, and on across the Serchio Valley to the IV

Corps boundary 6 miles east of the Serchio. The 2nd Battalion, 371st Infantry, was on the coastal plain one mile north of Forte dei Marmi, and the 3rd Battalion, 371st Infantry, was from Highway 1 just north of Querceta, through Seravezza to Azzano. The mountains were lightly held by the 92nd Cavalry Reconnaissance Troop. The 473rd Infantry garrisoned the Serchio Valley with the 1st Battalion, 371st Infantry, attached to hold the extreme right flank of the Division. The 370th Infantry had closed into its assembly area, under the cover of darkness, west of Highway 1 with its 1st Battalion prepared to spearhead the regimental attack.

During the night of 4 April, the 100th Battalion, 442nd Infantry, moved by truck under the cover of darkness, from their assembly area to the vicinity of Pietrasanta, dismounted and moved up to its line of departure on "Florida" hill mass, effecting the relief of elements of the 371st Infantry. The movement of the trucks, the dismount of the troops, the formation of the units, and movement forward to the line of departure was executed so quietly that it was barely noticed by the Assistant Chief of Staff G-3, standing 20 feet away.

The 3rd Battalion, 442nd Infantry, moved to Azzano then made an eight-hour climb up a precipitous zigzag trail on a treacherous shale-covered slope. The men, for the most part, crawled on hands and knees or pulled themselves up by low-growing shrub or the rifle butt of the man above. Several men were injured and one mule fell off the trail and was killed. During the night of 4 April, the 2nd Battalion, 473rd Infantry, moved by motor to an assembly area in the vicinity of Pozzi, as division reserve.

The offensive began at 0500 on 5 April after a series of air attacks on the Punta Bianca guns and other hostile positions. A ten-minute artillery preparation preceeded the jump off of the 1st Battalion, 370th Infantry, and the 100th Battalion, 442nd Infantry. Because of the eight-hour climb, the troops of the 3rd Battalion, 442nd Infantry, did not reach the Line of Departure until about 0530. However, the attack was in full swing by 0600, a little before dawn.

On the right flank, the 3rd Battalion, 442nd Infantry, launched its attack, making an enveloping movement around 2,800-foot Mount Folgorito from the east. The attack was launched without artillery preparation and achieved complete surprise. Gun positions were seized almost without a struggle, and enemy soldiers were killed or taken as prisoners. However, after the initial successes, the enemy was fully alert of the threat to his rear. Two hostile observation posts were destroyed with artillery fire. The drive to the summit of Mount Folgorito was temporarily halted by a counterattack and a rain of intensive artillery fire including fire from the Punta Bianca coastal guns. The attacking troops filtered through the fire by ones and twos and stormed the summit. In fierce hand-to-hand action, the enemy lost six dead and four captured while the remainder of the force escaped to the rear. In another action hostile 120-mm mortar fire killed three and wounded 20. The task of

The 100th Battalion, 442nd Infantry, moved by truck under the cover of darkness to the forward area and then by foot to the line of departure. These are men of the famous Nisei unit recruited in Hawaii and the western U.S. They were then sent to Italy as they were not trusted in the Pacific theater.

So, we went forward on the attack. . . . (Infantrymen moving at the crouch, rifle at the ready, with entrenching shovels hanging off of their web belts, ready to be used to dig in when required.)

supplying and evacuating was complicated by the terrain. By mid-afternoon the Division staff began to express concern that the 3rd Battalion may run out of ammunition. However, Col. Virgil R. Miller, Commander of 442nd Infantry, stated that in view of the relatively few casualties reported inflicted on the enemy by his 3rd Battalion, he was confident that they had ample ammunition. Rations, water, and ammunition had to be carried by packboard, a trip requiring eight hours to reach the forward elements. Italian porters, partisans, and all available personnel were pressed into service.

In the center, on the front of the 100th Battalion, 442nd Infantry, and 1st Battalion, 370th Infantry, the hostile positions were much more formidable and manned by a much more alert and determined force.

The 100th Battalion crossed the Line of Departure following a terrific artillery bombardment by the 599th and 329th Field Artillery Battalions, the Regimental Cannon Company, B Company, 895th Tank Destroyer Battalion, B Company, 84th Chemical Battalion (4.2 mortar), and the Assault Gun Platoon of the 758th Tank Battalion. Their initial objective was a knob of solid rock, containing at least 15 emplacements, and manned by a company of the enemy, known as "Georgia." Although it had been shelled and attacked over a five-month period, it had never been reduced. All day the battle raged at close hand grenade range with the attacking forces being subjected to trip mines, heavy artillery and mortar fire, and counterattacks. On one occasion, PFC Sadao M. Munemori, while leading an attack as acting squad leader, saw a grenade roll towards his helpless comrades. He rose into the withering fire, dove for the grenade, and smothered the blast with his own body. He was posthumously awarded the Medal of Honor. At midnight, the enemy mounted another strong counterattack. After an hour-long fire fight at close quarters the enemy fell back. The day's action cost the Germans 30 dead, 12 bunkers destroyed or captured, 17 machine guns and three 75-mm mountain howitzers captured, and several tons of ammunition and supplies taken intact. The price was high: 20 men killed and 123 wounded.

The artillery bombardment that preceded the attack of the 1st Battalion, 370th Infantry, was the heaviest delivered on the front of the 92nd Division. The attack was launched with two companies abreast: A Company on the right and C Company on the left. A Company moved forward rapidly occupying hill "X" and moved forward to hill "Y." The enemy counterattacked, disorganizing the company and killing its commander, Captain Dolranof. C Company was temporarily held up while a detail cleared a path through the mine field. Hostile fire and mine fields reduced the company to 25 men and four officers. The company was reorganized and continued its advance on the high ground east of Porta. In spite of increased resistance, heavy machine gun and mortar fire, Lieutenant Baker managed to secure the high ground west of Porta and dig in. Lieutenant Bailey, Company Commander for B Company, was killed shortly after it was committed to reinforce A Company. The 3rd Battalion attempting to move around to the right to capture Strettoia hill received brutal mortar fire. I and K Companies became disorganized. However, L Company supported by a tank platoon was able to make some

In the center of the Division sector, it was all up hill.

. . . And we took a few prisoners. An infantryman, with a Thompson sub-machine gun, brings in a jack-booted German prisoner.

progress. The 2nd Battalion was committed to pass through the 1st Battalion. After some confusion, the 2nd Battalion occupied hill "Y." It was, however, subsequently driven off by mortar and artillery fire and hostile counterattack. In view of his exposed right flank, Lieutenant Baker was ordered to withdraw by Capt. John F. Runyen, C Company Commander. Lieutenant Baker was subsequently awarded the Distinguished Service Cross. By nightfall, counterattacks had forced the 370th Infantry back to its original starting position after gaining some 2,000 yards. Four officers were killed and five were wounded. Ten enlisted men were killed and 109 were wounded. Fifteen enlisted men were missing in action.

During the night the 317th Engineer Battalion built a crossing across the Cinquale Canal, and Highway 1 was now open as far as Porta.

On 6 April the 100th and 3rd Battalions, 442nd Infantry, closed the pincers on the remaining enemy troops holding the "Ohio" peaks and Mount Cerretta. The 2nd Battalion was committed to action and gained Mount Folgorito during the night. While the 100th and 3rd Battalions were mopping up on Mount Cerretta and Mount Folgorito, the 2nd Battalion was encountering determined opposition from the crack Kesselring Machine Gun Battalion on Mount Belvedere. The Nazi battalion gave ground grudgingly and battered the attackers with a steady stream of mortar fire and concentrated fire from the guns on Punta Bianca. Hostile losses were heavy. The 442nd Infantry took 106 prisoners, mostly from the 281st Grenadier Regiment. This almost entirely eliminated the 1st Battalion of that Regiment.

The 2nd Battalion, 370th Infantry, scheduled to resume the attack at 0600 on 6 April, was unable to move forward due to the fact that the enemy had intercepted their radio messages giving the time of attack. A heavy mortar barrage was laid down on the battalion's avenue of approach at 0600. The attack was rescheduled for 0800, but radio monitors intercepted an enemy message stating that he was to be attacked at 0800 and that given reinforcements he could hold his position. A projected attack in the afternoon was called off after it was discovered that excessive straggling had reduced the battalion's effective strength to 88 men.

The 1st Battalion, 370th Infantry, was ordered to seize the high ground above Porta. However, before the attack could be launched, Capt. Donald M. Counts, commanding E Company, was killed. There was trouble getting the men into line and as darkness approached the attack was called off. The 3rd Battalion, 370th Infantry, remained in Regimental Reserve.

The left flank of the 442nd Infantry was now exposed to a depth of about 2½ miles. The right flank was also exposed, but was not so dangerous in that the terrain was extremely rough and the sector was garrisoned by low-grade Italian troops. Consequently, the 442nd Infantry devoted most of 7 April to consolidating and organizing the ground.

German equipment in cave on Monterumici Ridge.

Above and opposite: Germans had to be dug out of these defensive positions. In Italy the Germans were tenacious, defensive fighters, chose their positions well, and defended them stubbornly.

With two of the offensives of the 370th Infantry lagging, General Almond decided to commit his Divison Reserve, the 2nd Battalion, 473rd Infantry, to spearhead the 370th Infantry's attack on 7 April and to interchange the sector of the 370th and the 473rd Infantry Regiments. The 473rd would come to the Strettoia hills, and the 370th Infantry would take over the relatively quiet Serchio Valley sector. The 2nd Battalion, 473rd Infantry, now confronted the same determined hostile resistance on the enemy's Gothic Line that had

opposed the 370th Infantry. The enemy had excellent fields of fire and maximum observation. Artillery and mortar fires were poured against the hillsides in thundering barrages, and the enemy replied in kind. The only way to take Strettoia hill mass was for Infantry to root through each concrete and revetted foxhole.

While advancing between E and F Companies, Lt. Colonel Lisle was fatally wounded by hostile mortar fire. Maj. Robert W. Crandall took command of the 2nd Battalion, 473rd Infantry. The battalion gained about 1,650 yards seizing strong points in the Strettoia hill mass before becoming bogged down. The 2nd Battalion, 370th Infantry, relieved the 2nd Battalion, 371st Infantry, on the coastal plain, west of Highway 1. The 1st Battalion moved to the Serchio sector and relieved the 1st Battalion, 473rd Infantry, at midnight. The relieved unit moved to the coastal sector.

On 7 April, a task force of tanks and tank destroyers attempted to move up Highway 1. However, they were stopped by mine fields, bazookas, and fire from the coastal guns at Punta Bianca. The 2nd Battalion, 371st Infantry, joined the remainder of the Regiment in its move from the 92nd Division sector and came under the command of the IV Corps. The 371st Infantry was assigned to positions east of the zone of advance of the 92nd Division.

Lt. Col. John J. Phelan, Executive Officer, 370th Infantry, was placed in temporary command of the Serchio sector from midnight on 7 April until relieved by Col. Raymond G. Sherman, Commanding Officer, 370th Infantry, at noon on 8 April. With the following units, Colonel Sherman was directed to hold present position, patrol aggressively, and follow any enemy withdrawal without delay:

370th Infantry (less 2nd and 3rd Battalions, Anti-Tank Company, and I
   & R Platoon)
3rd Battalion, 473rd Infantry
111th Field Regiment (British)
17th Medium Regiment (less Q Battery-British)
A Company, 758th (Light) Tank Battalion
1st Platoon, B Company, 760th (Medium) Tank Battalion
92nd Reconnaissance Troop
Weapons Platoon, 758th (Light) Tank Battalion

Col. William P. Yarborough, Commanding Officer, 473rd Infantry (less 3rd Battalion), with the 3rd Battalion, 370th Infantry attached, was now in command of the former 370th Infantry sector.

On 8 April, the 3rd Battalion, 442nd Infantry, passed down the Colle Piano ridge line, occupied Montignoso and gathered up 16 prisoners on the way. The 2nd Battalion attacked Colle Tecchione, another spur of Mount Belvedere, and

A young German prisoner who had been told, "The Fuhrer said that the Japs were on our side," now is a prisoner of the Nisei.

Italians remove an anti-tank barrier, not only to facilitate movement for the Allies, but because the scrap was valuable.

came under constant artillery and mortar fire as well as small arms fire. After a three-hour fight, eight Germans were killed and six taken prisoner along with three machine guns and four mortars.

Two battalions of the 473rd Infantry were now committed in the Strettoia area. General Almond was not pleased with the advance of this Infantry Regiment, converted from anti-aircraft units. Accordingly, he relieved the two assault battalion commanders and four assault company commanders and replaced them with front line ("Follow Me") Infantrymen. Lt. Col. John J. Phelan, Regimental Executive Officer, 370th Infantry, assumed command of the 1st Battalion, and Maj. Robert H. Kirkwood, the 2nd Battalion. The results were like taking the brakes off. Both battalions began to move out.

Lt. Colonel Phelan started the uphill attack against hill 366 with B Company on the left and A Company on the right. Determined hostile resistance slowed the advance to a crawl. C Company, Battalion Reserve, was committed on 13 April. The final assault through heavy fire netted Sgt. Antonio Tanas and his squad 52 prisoners. However, before the position was completely consolidated, the hill was saturated with a heavy mortar and artillery barrage. One round landed in the doorway of a church being used as the battalion command post, killing Lt. Colonel Phelan and several others together with some prisoners of war. Colonel Sherman, Commanding Officer, 370th Infantry, was now in command of the Serchio Valley, and Colonel Yarborough, Commanding Officer, 473rd Infantry, was in command of the former 370th Infantry sector.

On 8 April, Lt. Colonel Arnold, Assistant Chief of Staff G-3, 92nd Division, on one of many visits to the leading elements discovered that the enemy had evacuated at Porta. After reconnoitering routes through the D-file, ahead of our leading elements, he ordered engineers forward to clear the road, deploying a portion of them, and directing their fire against hostile snipers so that the road-clearing could proceed. He then ordered forward the 760th Tank Battalion, the 758th Tank Battalion, the 895th Tank Destroyer Battalion, and the 3rd Battalion, 370th Infantry. When the D-file was intromitted by hostile artillery fire from the coastal guns at Punta Bianca, he was able to filter the force through the fire by one, two, or three vehicles at a time.

On 9 April, the 2nd Battalion, 442nd Infantry, on the right became engaged in a bitter battle for Pariana. Elements secured Altagnana and Pariana after heavy fighting. The 2nd Battalion then pushed on to the Frigido River line where they dug in on the south bank. The 3rd Battalion moved northwest along the slopes of Mount Belvedere against stiff resistance. The 100th Battalion, which had been protecting the regimental right and rear on Mount Folgorito, Mount Carchia, and Mount Belvedere, was released by the 2nd Battalion (less E Company), 370th Infantry. The relieved unit assembled in the vicinity of Altagnana as Regimental Reserve.

Men of 442nd Infantry run for cover from a German shell about to land, grabbing their helmets, and abandoning their wire-laying jeep. The fate of the lethargic driver is unknown.

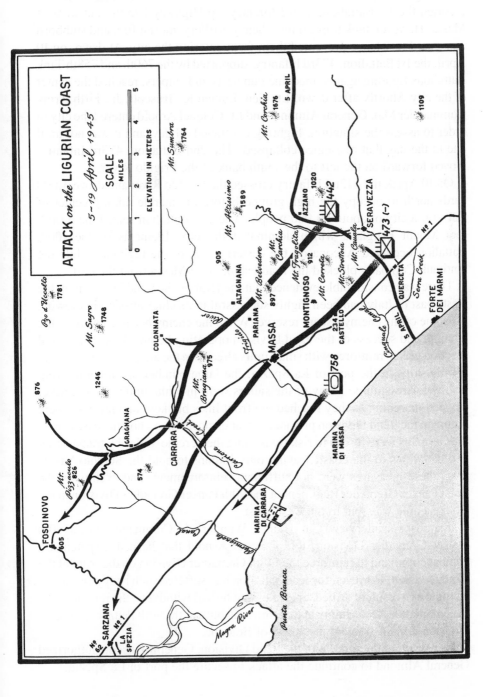

ATTACK on the LIGURIAN COAST

5-19 April 1945

SCALE
MILES
0 1 2 3 4 5

ELEVATION IN METERS

During the night, under the cover of darkness, the 760th Tank Battalion escorted the 1st Battalion, 473rd Infantry, up Highway 1 to the outskirts of Massa. However, tank traps, mines, heavy artillery, mortar fire, and stubborn rear guard resistance prevented them from entering the city. At dawn, on 10 April, the 1st Battalion, 473rd Infantry, supported by the 760th and 758th Tank Battalions fighting against machine gun nests and snipers, reached the center of the city. Shortly after dawn, Lt. Gen. Lucian K. Truscott, Jr., Fifth Army Commander Maj. General Almond, and Lt. Colonel Arnold entered the city in order to assess the situation. Fighting continued all day, and it was not until late in the day that resistance collapsed. The 2nd Battalion, 473rd Infantry, moved forward on the left to the south bank of the Frigido River.

On 10 April, the 442nd Infantry crossed the Frigido River and drove 3,000 yards north to occupy the high ground before the marble mining center of Carrara, a city of about 50,000 people. The 2nd Battalion seized the 3,000-foot Mount Brugiana which dominated the city. Elements of the 100th Battalion occupied Ancona on the eastern flank of the regiment while the Antitank Company blocked the road leading into Massa from the east.

There was considerable evidence that the feint by the 92nd Division on the west coast of Italy had been highly successful in its chief mission in drawing off some of the enemy's scant reserve. When the enemy became aware of the strength and success of the 92nd Division operating below Massa, his initial reaction was to reinforce with small units already in the area, including sailors off the ships in the port of La Spezia, the large number of line units from nearby fortress units. Many of the sailors were in white uniforms and never stopped marching as they reached the front lines but kept on until they were secure in the 92nd Division prisoner of war enclosures. As hostile losses grew, the Germans were forced to risk weakening the Serchio Valley by transferring two battalions to the coast, leaving only Italians to hold the Serchio Valley. Even these measures were not sufficient reinforcement, and eventually the 361st Panzer Grenadier Regiment of the 90th Panzer Grenadier Division in the Bologna area was sent to the west coast.

In a postwar interview, Col. Hans F. Wunderlich, Commander of the 90th Panzer Grenadier Division, told Colonel Arnold that he had dispatched a combat command to reinforce the 148th Grenadier Division on the front of the 92nd Division. However, the lead battalion had suffered such heavy casualties en route as a result of Allied air strikes that he had withdrawn the remainder of the command. Accordingly at that time, the bulk of the 90th Panzer Grenadier Division remained intact just north of Bologna.

As a result of the success of the 92nd Division, General Truscott authorized General Almond to continue the attack to secure the port of La Spezia.

15th Army Group Spring Offensive — the 92nd Division Attack

15th Army Group's plan anticipated that following the feint by the 92nd Division on its left, the Eighth Army, on its right, would resume the offensive on 10 April, with the Fifth Army, in the center, making the main effort starting on 14 April. With the long-awaited favorable weather, the time of the attack of the Eighth Army was subsequently changed to 9 April.

Following the heaviest air bombardment in the Mediterranean Theater and an artillery preparation, the V (British) Corps and II Polish Corps attacked across the Senio River at 7:20 p.m. with the V Corps on the right and II Polish Corps on the left. The V Corps attacked with the 8th Indian Division on the right and the 2nd New Zealand Division on the left. The II Polish Corps attacked with the 1st and 2nd Carpathian Brigades abreast. Heavy fighting continued through the day, with four enemy divisions — 42nd Jaeger, the 98th and 362nd Infantry, and the 26th Panzer Divisions — stubbornly resisting their advance.

Following the capture of Massa, the 92nd Division, under direct command of the Fifth Army, was ordered to continue the advance to capture La Spezia and hold the remainder of its front, patrolling aggressively, and follow up any enemy without delay.

The Division now stood face-to-face with the Green Line. In addition to the 281st and 285th Grenadier Regiments, the coastal sector was defended by at least one battalion of the 286th Grenadier Regiment, the 4th High Mountain Battalion, the 1048th Engineer Battalion, the 907th Fortress Battalion, the 1st Battalion, 361st Panzer Grenadier Regiment, plus marines, sailors, and service troops from La Spezia supported by the coastal guns on Punta Bianca, all with order to defend their positions until death.

In an effort to speed the advance, General Almond narrowed the zone of the 473rd Infantry by assigning the flat land between the coast and Highway 1 to a special task force of tanks and infantry. This Task Force, under the command of Lt. Col. Claire S. Curtis and known as TF-Curtis, consisted of the 758th Tank Battalion (less A Company); Headquarters and B Company, 760th Tank Battalion; A Company, 894th Tank Destroyer Battalion; E Company, 370th Infantry; and Anti-Tank Company, 473rd Infantry. TF-Curtis was given the mission of clearing the coastal sector west of Massa.

The 473rd Infantry (less 3rd Battalion) was ordered to continue its attack and capture the port of La Spezia. The 442nd Infantry was directed to continue its attack and capture the important road junction of Aulla, northeast of La Spezia. The 370th Infantry (less 2nd Battalion), with the 3rd Battalion, 473rd Infantry, attached, was directed to hold its position in the Serchio sector at all cost, patrol aggressively, and follow any enemy withdrawal. The 2nd Battalion, 370th Infantry, with the attached 1st Platoon, 92nd Reconnaissance Troop, was to fill the mountainous gap between the 442nd and 370th Infantries. Massa was now outflanked from the east by the 442nd Infantry.

Attempts by the 473rd Infantry to force a crossing of the Frigido, on the afternoon of 10 April, were fiercely contested until the 2nd Battalion commander brought up a platoon of the 894th Tank Destroyer Battalion, placed them on high ground above the river, and had them fire all afternoon on the numerous enemy guns in houses on the north bank. The battalion was able to complete its crossing after dark and repulsed the enemy's immediate counterattack. The 1st Battalion met strong resistance, so that its efforts to cross the Frigido River were delayed until noon on 11 April. Despite fighter-bomber attacks, the Punta Bianca coastal guns shelled the crossings and Massa continually.

On 10 April, the 442nd Infantry crossed the Frigido River. The 3rd Battalion, on the left, moved rapidly ahead through the foothills above the coastal plain. The 2nd Battalion seized 3,000 feet of Mount Brugiana which dominated the city of Carrara. The 100th Battalion, on the right, occupied Ancona, and Anti-Tank Company blocked the road leading into Massa from the east.

The 3rd Battalion moved down on Carrara on 11 April and found the city in complete control of the partisans. Also, elements of the Battalion also took Gragnana and Sorgnano without opposition. The 100th Battalion continued over nearly impossible terrain and occupied the mountain hamlet of Colonnata, three miles east of Carrara. Other units occupied the outskirts of Carrara until 473rd Infantry advanced far enough to cover its flanks.

The 370th Infantry (less 2nd Battalion) continued active patrolling in the

Serchio sector. TF-Curtis inched forward as it was subjected to heavy fire from the high ground on the right flank and from enemy guns on Punta Bianca. Resupplying became critical for the 442nd Infantry and to a lesser extent for the 473rd Infantry, for the Massa-Carrara road was rendered impassable by mines, craters, and artillery fire. Four bulldozers of the 232nd Combat Engineers, attempting to repair the road on 11 April, were destroyed by mines and artillery fire. Ravines, cliffs, and peaks prevented movement of carrying parties, making it necessary to drop supplies from airplanes.

Enemy resistance, including aggressive raids, increased at Carrione Creek indicating that he had reached another in his series of well-prepared positions of his Green Line defenses. Heavy artillery concentrations on other parts of the front indicated that the Germans intended to end their withdrawal. To offset his heavy losses he had been forced to call upon most of his available reserves. One company each of the 1048th Engineer Battalion and the 907th Fortress Battalion had been committed. Both were virtually destroyed. The 1st Battalion, 281st Grenadier Regiment, had sustained casualties to the extent that it was pulled out of the line, reorganized with the addition of 100 Air Force replacements, and recommitted.

An attempt by TF-Curtis to force a crossing of Carrione Creek on 13 April was repulsed by heavy small arms and anti-tank fire covering strong anti-tank obstacles. However, the 473rd Infantry, although held up on the right flank by concrete pillboxes, succeeded in pushing A Company to within two miles of the Parmignola Canal.

The 442nd Infantry continued the attack with the 2nd Battalion on the right and the 100th Battalion on the left. The 3rd Battalion was in Regimental Reserve in the vicinity of Carrara. As the 2nd Battalion attacked toward Mount Pizzaculo, it was suddenly hit with air bursts from hostile artillery and self-propelled guns. The fire was so intense that the battalion was forced to dig in for the night. Enemy artillery fire also halted the advance of the 100th Battalion. Our artillery was not yet within range of the mountain, having been outdistanced by the regiment's rapid advance.

In the coastal sector, the enemy covered his withdrawal with increasingly effective artillery fire, particularly from the coastal guns at Punta Bianca. Both Massa and Carrara were repeated targets of heavy enemy concentrations, as were all of the avenues of approach in the coastal sector.

Brig. Gen. William H. Colbern, Commanding General, 92nd Division Artillery, coordinated the use of his 155-mm guns in suppressing hostile anti-aircraft batteries protecting the coastal guns at Punta Bianca with almost daily attacks on the guns by fighter-bombers and medium bombers of the Air Corps. However, these air attacks had no effect on the operations of the Punta Bianca guns. This was the case until 14 April, when the leading elements of our attacking forces had advanced sufficiently to permit our artillery to come into

Prisoners are moved to the rear.

range. All 36 of the 76-mm guns of the 679th Tank Destroyer Battalion were assigned to neutralize the coastal pieces. The ports of the coastal guns were covered by steel doors that were opened to permit the guns to fire. Each time an enemy gun fired, it received 60 to 180 high velocity rounds, aimed at the ports, from the tank destroyers. The first rounds landed within 45 seconds after the forward observer saw gun smoke and called for fire. The enemy's smoke generator, used to screen his positions, was destroyed on 15 April. Hostile self-propelled guns which attempted to duel with the tank destroyers were knocked out. An eight-inch howitzer was brought up to help deal with the Punta Bianca guns. However, the only effective weapons were the tank destroyer guns. By 19 April, all of the guns on the east side of Punta Bianca had been neutralized.

Fifth Army launched the main attack of 15 Army Group on 14 April. At 0945, the IV Corps jumped off with three divisions and two Infantry regiments detached from the 92nd Division. The 365th Infantry was employed in the Cutigliano area and the 371st Infantry southwest of Mount Belvedere. The II Corps was started by the 88th Division and the 6th South African Armored Division at 2230 with the main effort directed towards the capture of Bologna.

While the Fifth Army offensive was gaining momentum on Highway 64 to the east of the 92nd Division sector, TF-Curtis crossed Carrione Creek on 15 April. Their tanks began to roll by noon on the 16th. Progress was slow in the remainder of the coastal sector. The 473rd and 442nd Infantry Regiments moved forward from feature to feature in the high ground adjoining the coastal plain. In the Serchio sector, the 370th Infantry continued active patrolling. Fiattone was occupied on 16 April, without opposition. Indications pointed to an enemy withdrawal in the sector. Patrols probed aggressively into the enemy lines. Combat patrols entered and occupied Campo and Bechelli on 17 April.

Along Highway 1, the 473rd Infantry crossed the Parmignola Canal on 17 April and closed in on Sarzana, at the junction of Highway 1 and 62. On the right of the coastal sector, the 442nd Infantry tried again and again to pierce the enemy's defenses running north and south from the mountain strongpoint of Fosdinovo, but gains were small. After three days of heavy fighting, hill 706 and Mount Grugola fell. The advance continued slowly against stubborn resistance and intense artillery fire.

Withdrawal of the enemy in the Serchio sector on the night of 18 April was closely followed by a general advance by the 370th Infantry. On 19 April, strong combat patrols pushed forward, and the important road junction and communications center of Castelnuovo was occupied shortly after dawn the next day. At about the same time, Colonel Arnold, while accompanying Colonel Sherman, 370th Infantry Commander, surprised an enemy machine gun position and captured four prisoners of war.

The 3rd Battalion, 473rd Infantry, was detached from the 370th Infantry and joined its parent regiment on the morning of 20 April. The 2nd Battalion, 370th Infantry, operating in the area between the coastal and the Serchio sectors, occupied Mount Antona and Mount Altissimo on 20 April.

The 370th Infantry continued its advance to the northeast against light resistance. Numerous mines and obstacles along the road slowed the advance. Small delaying detachments were encountered and reduced. On 22 April, the 1st Battalion encountered more determined resistance in the vicinity of Camporgiano. A captured enemy Field Order and reconnaissance of other points showed this to be one point of the enemy's new main line of resistance, which was in the process of being organized. Accordingly, it was evident that speed was essential. The battalion immediately deployed and outflanked this position. Under the cover of darkness, on the night of 23 April, the 3rd Battalion was assembled from widely-scattered points high in the mountains, mounted on trucks, moved approximately 15 miles, dismounted, and marched about five miles over a mountain pass. At dawn on 23 April, they were at Gramolazzo and along the enemy's next planned line of resistance before they could get there. The 3rd Battalion pushed on during that day to Casala which was held by a small German garrison. They surrounded the town and, after a brief fire fight, captured two officers and 24 enlisted men. The 2nd Battalion, 370th Infantry, after a two-day march over very precipitous terrain, made contact with its parent regiment and moved to Gragnola.

On 20 April, the 3rd Battalion, 442nd Infantry, encountered stiff enemy resistance in the vicinity of Fosdinovo and Tendola. All units of the regiment advanced slowly against determined enemy resistance. Progress may have been better if the troops had been fresh. However, most were dead tired from two weeks of operation over the high North Apennines Mountains.

On 21 April, both the 100th and 2nd Battalions attacked at 0800 along Golle Musatello ridge line. Progress was very slow. The ridge was defended by the fresh troops of the 3rd Battalion, 361st Panzer Grenadier Regiment, 90th Panzer Grenadier Division. Leading the attack was 2nd Lt. Daniel K. Inouye. He first led his platoon in a rapid encirclement that resulted in the destruction of a German mortar observation post and brought them close to hostile positions dug into rock crevices. The platoon was pinned down by crossfire from three machine guns. Lieutenant Inouye crawled to within five yards of the nearest gun and tossed two grenades into the nest. He then stood up and destroyed the second gun crew with fire from his submachine gun. He was hit in the abdomen by a bullet which came out of his back, barely missing his spine. He continued to lead his platoon and advanced alone against a machine gun position which had his men pinned down. He tossed two grenades with devastating effect before his right arm was shattered by a German rifle grenade at close range. He threw his last grenade with his left hand, attacked

The 92nd Division enters La Spezia.

The 92nd Division enters La Spezia.

The 92nd Division enters La Spezia.

Partisans parade in La Spezia — these were Italian patriots who had been operating as armed civilians behind the German lines, sometimes as rival political bands.

Partisans in La Spezia.

with a submachine gun and was finally knocked down the hill by a bullet in his leg. He spent 20 months in Army hospitals after losing his arm. In the attack, 25 Germans were killed and eight captured. Lieutenant Inouye received the Distinguished Service Cross.[6]

The 3rd Battalion attacked on the morning of 23 April, and after heavy fighting, secured Mount Nebbione and Tendola. Following this, the battalion successfully repulsed three separate 40-man counterattacks. The 2nd Battalion attacked to the northwest from positions in the vicinity of South Terenzo on 23 April and, after heavy fighting on the outskirts, captured the important communications center and stronghold in the Gothic Line of Aulla, at the junction of Highways 62 and 63 on the morning of 24 April.

On 24 April, the 1st Battalion, 370th Infantry, occupied Fivizzano and pushed on against light resistance to Luccianna. The 3rd Battalion relieved elements of the 442nd Infantry in Aulla and moved on to occupy Terrarossa. The 442nd Infantry assembled west of Carrara as Division Reserve.

After the 3rd Battalion, 473rd Infantry, completed its move from the Serchio sector on 20 April, the 1st Battalion went into Regimental Reserve. The 2nd and 3rd Battalions continued the attack against strong enemy resistance south of Sarzana. Hostile artillery continued to be intense. Little progress was made during the next two days. On 22 April, the 1st Battalion relieved the 2nd Battalion. The 1st and 3rd Battalions continued to advance against slackening resistance. Although battered, the hostile forces were not shattered. Supporting fires from the 92nd Division Artillery crashed in Sarzana and the enemy responded by throwing his "grand piano" shells (305-mm) into CPs near Caniparola and anything that moved on Highway 1. However, the advance was continued and Sarzana, S. Stefano, and Caprigliola were occupied. Hostile forces began to withdraw in haste. Sarzana was taken with negligible opposition.

Now the race was on. The tank-infantry column of TF-Curtis, consisting of Maj. Lawrence F. Becnel's 758th Tank Battalion, reinforced with E Company, 370th Infantry, crossed the Magra River to Po, moved up Highway 1, crossed the Magra to Punta Bianca on 22 April, with 1st Lt. Earl Heggett's 473rd Infantry I and R Platoon leading the way. The race ended quickly when reconnaissance found an enemy delaying force in the factory area at the southern outskirts of S. Stefano. The Germans fought for a few hours on the evening of 23 April and then pulled back to Aulla.

As hostile resistance began to give way and forward reconnaissance became more than "hold your helmet at arm's length to test for bullet-holes," Lieutenant Heggetts' I and R Platoon successfully patrolled into La Spezia and found the partisans in control of the city. Headquarters 473rd Infantry moved into the offices in La Spezia before 0800, which had been occupied by the German command the day before. About half an hour later, the Italian

Street scene in La Spezia at the end of the war showing young partisan commanders, well-armed, and an OSS officer in a USAAF uniform exchanging remarks, near a captured enemy car.

Street scene in
La Spezia.

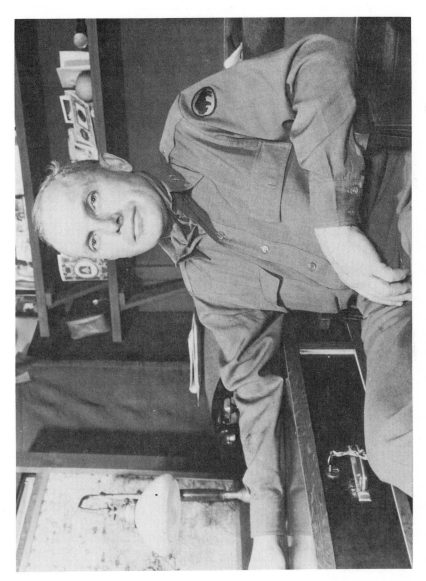

Maj. Gen. Edward M. Almond, Commanding General, 92nd Division, in his mobile office.

stenographers reported to work. A number of them went into anterooms, removed their clothing, and donned robes (ready for the morning's activity of close liaison) before they realized that the offices were occupied by Americans. German forces had fallen back to the high ground of La Force, a suburb on the northwest side of the city. Task Force Steinman, consisting of the 92nd Division Reconnaissance Troop and a platoon of the 473rd Anti-Tank Company as infantry moved into La Spezia on the night of 23-24 April.

On the morning of 24 April, the 1st Battalion, 473rd Infantry, moved through S. Stefano, crossed the Magra River, and seized the high ground two miles northwest of the city without firing a shot. The 3rd Battalion, on the right, hiked through the hills north of S. Stefano without opposition. The 2nd Battalion encountered about 50 marines with six 20-mm guns at La Force. Two guns of the Cannon Company, supporting the 2nd Battalion, engaged the 20-mm guns in a direct fire duel and knocked out three. G Company captured the remaining and eliminated the enemy position. Late on 24 April, the remainder of the 473rd Infantry assembled and moved into La Spezia, and the Regiment prepared for operations towards Genoa.

After the breakthrough of the Gothic Line and the capture of La Spezia on 24 April, the 92nd Division planned to pursue the enemy north and west.

On 24 April, Gen. Mark W. Clark, Commanding 15th Army Group, placed the 92nd Division directly under his operational control and authorized it to continue its attack. That afternoon, the Division issued Field Order No. 11 directing: Combat Team 473, including the 598th Field Artillery Battalion, C Company, 760th Medium Tank Battalion; A Company, 594th Tank Destroyer Battalion (-1 Platoon); B Company, 317th Engineer Combat Battalion; C Collecting Company, 317th Medical Battalion, and the Assault Gun Platoon, 758th Light Tank Battalion, to pursue the enemy west and seize Genoa; Combat Team 370th including 597th Field Artillery Battalion, 111th (British) Field Artillery Regiment, 1st Platoon, A Company, 758th Light Tank Battalion, and the 1st Platoon, A Company, 894th Tank Destroyer Battalion to pursue the enemy north on Highways 62 and 63 to the limit of Cisa Pass-Cerreta Pass; the 92nd Reconnaissance Troop to reconnoiter in zone bypassing enemy resistance and report crossing phase lines; 442nd Infantry Regiment to assemble in Division Reserve and be prepared to make an amphibious envelopment. Lt. Colonel Arnold was relieved of his duties as Assistant Chief of Staff, G-3, and placed in command of the 598th Field Artillery Battalion. Lt. Col. Edward L. Rowny became the new Assistant Chief of Staff, G-3.

THE PURSUIT

By the time La Spezia and Aulla had been captured, the enemy was badly disorganized in the western sector. The 51st Mountain Corps, limited in mobility by the lack of transport and fuel, attempted to extract itself from the mountains southwest of Parma. The enemy continued to withdraw, leaving behind small delaying forces and large quantities of materiel.

Remnants of the German 148th Grenadier Division, supported by 361st Panzer Grenadier Regiment (less 1 battalion), 70th Panzer Grenadier Division, remnants of the 4th High Mountain Battalion, and remnants of the Italia Division, held most of the area in front of the 92nd Division. Hostile units between La Spezia and Genoa included the 135th Fortress Brigade, about 500 miscellaneous Italian units in isolated garrisons, and about 500 of the La Spezia garrison. The Genoa-Savona area was known to be a fascist stronghold and the seat of the German naval command in northwest Italy. Italian troops included a blackshirt brigade of about 1,500 and about 1,000 miscellaneous troops. The total strength of the Germans in the area was about 4,000, with the 7th Marine Security Division alone consisting of about 1,800. Other enemy reserves which could influence the action included the 34th Infantry Division from the Ligurian coast west of Genoa, and the 5th Mountain Division. Elements of the Littoria, San Marco, and Monte Rosa Italian Divisions were in the area west and northwest of Genoa.

Eighth Army continued to advance along the Adriatic coast against determined resistance. By 23 April, the Po River was reached by both flanks of the V Corps, but in the center the enemy continued to fight stubbornly for Ferrara. Bologna fell to the Fifth Army with unexpected ease on the morning of 21 April and the Army continued to drive towards the Po River. The German line was broken, and the hostile forces were split in two.

Brig. Gen. Donald W. Braun, Assistant Chief of Staff, G-3, of the 15th Army Group, met with General Almond just before the 473rd Combat Team

Rapallo, Sta. Margherita, Pareggi, and Porto Fino. Typical small Italian west coast resort towns, on the road to Genoa, very popular with European tourists. From a military point of view, the country is difficult with only a very narrow coastal road, steep cliffs, and mountains behind.

began its advance from La Spezia to Genoa at dawn on 25 April. General Almond made him a wager that the advance of over 110 miles would take less than four days. Screened by the 92nd Reconnaissance Troop and the 473rd's I and R Platoons, the Regimental Combat Team began its advance up Highway 1 with tanks of the 760th Tank Battalion and the 894th Tank Destroyer Battalion in the lead, followed by the 2nd Battalion, 473rd Infantry, riding on tanks, tank destroyers, jeeps, and trucks, followed by the 598th Field Artillery Battalion.

Colonel Arnold raced forward behind the column in his jeep picking up batteries of the 598th Field Artillery Battalion and dropping them off so as to have at least one battery in position at all times to provide supporting fires, as required. The 1st Battalion, 473rd Infantry, cleared the area between Highway 1 and the sea. The 3rd Battalion followed in Regimental Reserve.

The initial advance of the column was extremely rapid through the mountains. As previously arranged by Lt. Col. Donald M. MacWillie, Assistant Chief of Staff G-2, partisans had seized control of all of the bridges and prevented German demolition detachments from destroying them, thus keeping them open for the advancing troops. However, Highway 1 dropped down from the mountains in the vicinity of Sestrilevante with mountains on one side and the sea on the other, except where it passed through a series of tunnels. As the column emerged from one tunnel, between Sestrilevante and Lavagna, it was caught on the road and heavily shelled by coastal guns at Porto Fino. The column was able to continue its advance by rapid movement from one tunnel to the next between hostile artillery concentrations.

Small arms resistance was encountered in Lavagna from hostile forces defending a stream. Troops of the 2nd Battalion, 473rd Infantry, dismounted, crossed the stream, and quickly subdued the resistance. The march was resumed. However, a short time later it advanced against a more determined resistance along a creek line on the eastern edge of Chiavari. The 2nd Battalion again dismounted and some elements were successful in crossing the creek, but their advance was stopped by hostile enfilade fire and heavy artillery concentrations from 135-mm coastal defense guns above the hillside tunnel at Chiavari, 152-mm coastal defense guns at Porto Fino, and field artillery batteries. Maj. Robert Crandall, Commanding Officer, 2nd Battalion, 473rd Infantry, was killed as was Capt. Murray Steinman, Commanding Officer, 92nd Reconnaissance Troop. In addition to the personnel losses, reconnaissance vehicles, twelve jeeps, several trucks, and other equipment were destroyed. Capt. David Streger assumed command of the 2nd Battalion. At that time, because of the rapid advance of the column, it had outdistanced the range of its supporting artillery. The only heavy supporting fire available was from two tanks of the 760th Tank Battalion. These boldly sought to engage the enemy guns firing from the tunnel mouth above Chiavari.

Later in the day, the 598th Field Artillery Battalion, also having been subjected to heavy artillery concentrations on the road from Sestrilevante to Lavagna, occupied firing positions at street intersections and other open areas between Lavagna and Chiavari and, by dusk, had silenced the last four hostile 135-mm batteries and destroyed one six-inch battery, but the cost to our forces was heavy.

After a period of reorganization, the 2nd Battalion, with tanks of the 760th Tank Battalion in the lead, resumed its advance at dawn on 26 April, in spite of extensive hostile mines left in the area. The charred remains of an extensive hostile troop billet area was found inside of the Chiavari tunnel. Also in the tunnel was one of the destroyed naval guns.

The advancing troops entered Rapallo without opposition and drove into a group of confused Italian Fascists who promptly surrendered. Later, in the beautiful city of Sta. Margherita, the surrender of a company of Germans was accepted.

Later, the advancing column was again halted on the high ground of the mountain ridge between Sta. Margherita and Camogli. The 598th Field Artillery Battalion occupied firing positions in Santa Margherita. The three firing batteries dug in on three tennis courts, the only available open ground. Battalion Headquarters occupied Contessa Edda Mussolini Ciano's (Mussolini's daughter) villa. Fire was delivered on suspected hostile positions on the ridge line. An anti-tank gun knocked out the lead tank of the 760th Tank Battalion wounding the driver. A tank-infantry team was assembled to take out the anti-tank gun.

The advance towards Genoa was resumed on the morning of 27 April. A last ditch resistance was encountered on the edge of the city when the column reached a roadblock established by the German Marine Garrison of Genoa. The German Marines had established an ambush by fortifying a defile leading into the city of Villa Paradiso. The U.S. advance was halted. All of the tanks were buttoned up and unable to advance. When Lt. Colonel Arnold reached the head of the column, he was the only one in an exposed position. He quickly assembled a small detachment, made up primarily of artillerymen, and assaulted the position, forcing the surrender of 280 German Marines at 1000 on 27 April.

While the Marine prisoners were being assembled, and present explosive charges were being removed from Villa Paradiso, the column moved into the city which was in the hands of the partisans. As a show of force, the column was to march through the city. Some of the troops of the 2nd Battalion boarded streetcars and rode to the western part of the town. As the 598th Field Artillery Battalion reached the park area, it came under small arms fire from upper windows of adjacent buildings. Lt. Colonel Arnold ordered that trails be dropped and nearby buildings taken under fire. However, General Almond, arriving at that time, directed that the battalion withdraw to positions of

Villi Pareggi, near Porto Fino, occupied by General Almond at the end of the war.

readiness.

In the western part of the city, partisans had divided and surrounded the enemy garrison of about 4,000 men under the command of the German Maj. General Meinhold. A garrison of 700 Germans, west of the harbor entrance, surrendered in the afternoon, and 259 Germans, at the east end of the entrance to the harbor, surrendered shortly thereafter. The 3rd Battalion, 473rd Infantry, received the surrender of nearly 3,000 troops at Uscio and Ferrada, northeast of Genoa. The 1st Battalion accepted the surrender of the Giovi garrison. Small detachments of the 135th Fortress Brigade, commanded by Maj. General Meinhold, surrendered to various units. The 473rd Infantry established a prisoner of war stockade in the athletic stadium in Genoa. The advance had been completed in less than three days, and General Almond had won his wager with Brig. General Braun.

One German garrison refused to surrender. This was the Coast Artillery Unit on Mount Moro that overlooked Genoa and the Mediterranean. On the night of 27 April, Colonel Yarborough, 473rd Combat Team Commander, expressed some concern for the safety of the approximately 1,200 U.S. troops in Genoa. Approximately 4,000 hostile forces were in the hands of partisans, about 3,000 were being held by U.S. forces, and an estimated 3,000 coast artillerymen ringing the city had not surrendered. Lt. Colonel Arnold assured him that the nature of coast artillerymen was such that they would never leave their guns and fight as infantrymen if they could possibly help it.

The Cannon Company, 473rd Infantry, attached to the 598th Field Artillery Battalion, was deployed to the high ground of Mount Moro to fire directly on some of the coast artillery positions. The German Commander, a major, waved a white flag and asked to be permitted to remain by his guns until the war was officially ended. His request was refused.

That night, under the direction of Brig. Gen. William H. Colbern, 92nd Division Artillery Commander, 12 guns of A Company, 679th Tank Destroyer Battalion, were moved forward to approximately 400 yards' range for direct fire on the German guns. By daylight, they were ready to fire. Additionally, all guns of the 598th Field Artillery Battalion were in position 1,200 yards west of Mount Moro and prepared for direct fire on the enemy guns. Also, all guns of the 600th Field Artillery Battalion were in position 3,000 yards southeast of Mount Moro and ready to fire. Further negotiations with the German commander resulted in Brig. General Colbern directing that an ultimatum be given to surrender by noon on 28 April. With about five minutes to spare, the German commander surrendered to the 473rd Infantry. The total number of prisoners was now 11,553.

While the 473rd Regimental Combat Team was advancing on Genoa, the 370th Regimental Combat Team was driving toward the Cisa Pass and Cerreta Pass on Highways 62 and 63. The 148th Grenadier Division and the Italia

Division withdrew before them to the north to avoid being captured. On 24 April, the 1st Battalion, 370th Infantry, moved northeast from Aulla to Fivizzano, on Highway 63. From there, a company moved to the northwest and captured Licciana. Other elements of the Battalion continued northeast on Highway 63 and took possession of Cerreto Pass and pushed out patrols as far as Reggio, where Highway 63 joined Highway 9. At Reggio, contact was made with the Brazilian Expeditionary Force.

The 3rd Battalion, 370th Infantry, moved to the north along Highway 62 and reached Pontremoli and the Cisa Pass on 26 April. The enemy fought a strong delaying action until the advancing troops reached the outskirts of Pontremoli, where they organized their positions on dominant terrain for a final stand. The advance of the 3rd Battalion was halted by machine guns, small arms, artillery, mortars, and direct fire from self-propelled guns and tanks. With the assistance of about 1,000 partisans, the enemy was driven out of the city on 28 April. Approximately 300 prisoners and much equipment were captured. On 29 April, the 148th Grenadier Division withdrew beyond Cisa Pass, into the sector of the Brazilian Expedition Force, and surrendered the Maj. General Mascarenja's troops.

On 29 April, the 2nd Battalion, 370th Infantry, assumed responsibility for all tunnels on Highway 1 between Sestrilevante and Genoa with a minimum of four guards at each tunnel.

On 27 April, the 442nd Infantry moved from its Division Reserve position to Chiavari and then proceeded to outflank Genoa from the north. The 3rd Battalion moved along Highway 45, entered Genoa, and contacted the 473rd Infantry there. The Battalion arrived in style. Lt. Colonel Alfred A. Pursall, 3rd Battalion Commander, having stopped ten street cars on the outskirts of the city, had his troops board the street cars and ride to the western part of the city which they garrisoned, together with the high ground to the north and west.

The 100th Battalion, 442nd Infantry, continued its march to the northwest and reached Busalla in the mountain pass which led from Genoa to the Po River. Patrols were pushed out. Isola del Cantone was outposed with tanks and infantry. The 2nd Battalion, 442nd Infantry, continued its march in tanks and trucks to the north and northwest, having begged, borrowed, and stolen enough gasoline to make the trip. Contact was made with elements of IV Corps in Pavia and with the Brazilians in Alessandria, both cities in the Po Valley. In Alessandria, about 1,000 Germans surrendered without a struggle. Asti, the champagne center of Italy, was occupied shortly thereafter. The local products were used to celebrate the liberation.

On 30 April, the 442nd Intelligence and Reconnaissance Platoon, led by Lt. Robert I. Wakuya, and a machine gun section from H Company, accompanied by Col. William J. McCaffrey, Chief of Staff, 92nd Division, made a 75-mile

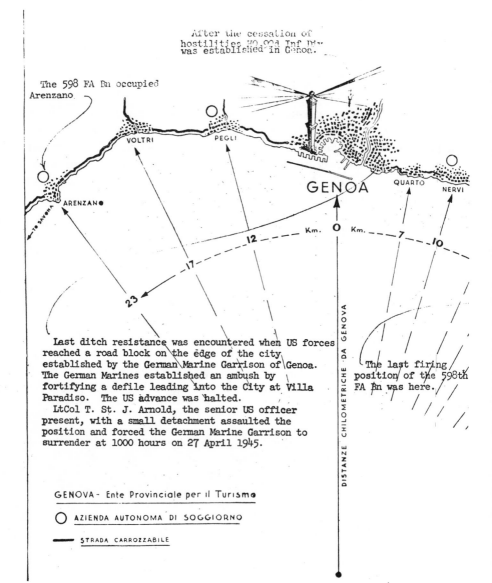

After the cessation of
hostilities HQ 92d Inf Div
was established in Genoa.

The 598 FA Bn occupied
Arenzano

VOLTRI   PEGLI

GENOA   QUARTO   NERVI

ARENZANO

TO SAVONA

12 ----- Km. 0 Km. ---- 7 ---- 10

17

23

DISTANZE CHILOMETRICHE DA GENOVA

Last ditch resistance was encountered when US forces
reached a road block on the edge of the city
established by the German Marine Garrison of Genoa.
The German Marines established an ambush by
fortifying a defile leading into the City at Villa
Paradiso. The US advance was halted.
LtCol T. St. J. Arnold, the senior US officer
present, with a small detachment assaulted the
position and forced the German Marine Garrison to
surrender at 1000 hours on 27 April 1945.

The last firing
position of the 598th
FA Bn was here.

GENOVA - Ente Provinciale per il Turismo

O AZIENDA AUTONOMA DI SOGGIORNO

━━ STRADA CARROZZABILE

After the breakthrough of the German Gothic Line and the capture of LaSpezia by the 92d Inf. Div on 24 April 1945, MajGen Almond ('15) ordered the 3d Bn 473 Infantry and the 598th FA Bn, commanded by LtCol Arnold ('35) to advance along the Ligurian Coast as rapidly as possible and capture Genoa.

RAPALLO

SORI

RECCO

ZOAGLI

CAMOGLI

S. MARGHERITA
LIGURE

16 20 22 31 32 36 37

PORTOFINO

CHIAVARI

LAVAGNA

45 46 53

SESTRI LEVANTE

TO LA SPEZIA

After the capture of Genoa, Castello Parrago was used as MajGen Almond's Villa.

3d Bn 473 Inf and 598 FA Bn were caught on the road and heavily shelled by guns from Portofino on 25 April 1945. All Infantry field grade Officers were casualties.

The lines were established along this creek on 25 April 1945.

The 598 FA Bn neutralized the last four enemy batteries on 25 April 1945. One 6" battery was destroyed here.

Over 128 major ships were on the bottom of the harbor of Genoa when the 92nd Division arrived.

The 92nd Division arrives in Genoa.

The 92nd Division arrives in Genoa.

The 92nd Division arrives in Genoa.

598th Field Artillery Battalion enters Genoa.

dash to Torino. However, the German 75th Corps, in the area, refused to surrender to such a small force. The platoon was also dispatched to Casala. Roadblocks were established on all main routes leading to and from Genoa. The 473rd Infantry, Intelligence and Reconnaissance Platoon, moved down Highway 1, along the coast, and made contact with the French at Imperia. The 598th Field Artillery Battalion moved down the coast to Arenzana.

On 29 April, Benito Mussolini was captured and executed by partisans in the mountains of Northern Italy. He was making a run for the Swiss border. His body, together with that of his mistress, Clara Petacci, was brought to Milan and hung upside down in a service station in Milan's Piazza Loreto. Germans and Italians surrendered by the thousands, and the prisoner of war problem was complicated by the fact that most of the evacuations had to be done on foot. In addition, the enemy yielded an overwhelming amount of materiel. The 92nd Division captured a total of 13,630 prisoners of war during the month of April 1945. Its losses during the month were 11 killed, 380 wounded, and 1,517 missing in action.

On 29 April, two German officers, a lieutenant colonel on behalf of Gen. Heinrich von Vietinghoff, Commander-in-Chief, Southwest, and a major on behalf of SS Gen. Karl Wolff, Supreme Commander of SS and Police Troops and Plenipotentiary General of the Wehrmacht in Italy, signed the surrender agreement at Allied Force Headquarters in the Royal Palace at Caserta, Italy. According to this agreement, the war in Italy ended on 2 May 1945. The German armies which had fought so skillfully and bitterly from Salerno to the Po were finished.

THE CITY

Initial location of HQ 92d Inf Div in Genoa

14" Coastal guns were in position on the mountains on either side of Genoa. German Personnel manning these guns did not surrender until late on 27 April 1945. The Cannon Company of the 34th FA Bn was deployed to fire direct fire on some of these positions

...as first area ...t ... ...y 1500, 27 April 1945,

This position was fortified by 280 German Marines. The position was invaded by Lt Col. Arnold (335) and the garrison surrendered to him at 1008 hours 27 April 1945

The 34th FA Bn occupied positions here on the night of 27 April 1945. There were approximately 1200 troops in Genoa at that time. Approximately all German had surrendered and about 3000 had not

The second location of HQ 92d Inf Div in Genoa

Supplies were unloaded from landing crafts.

...ducted ...c map 1945, ...Columbus ...s to the ...place.

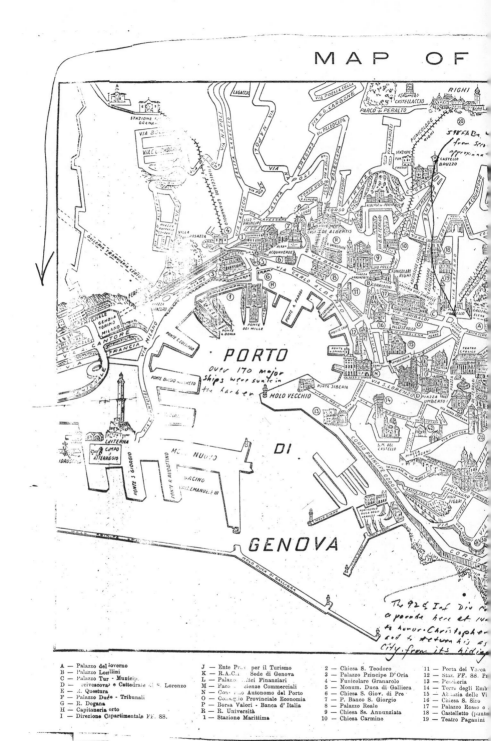

PORTO

Over 170 major ships were sunk in the harbor

DI

GENOVA

MOLO VECCHIO

*The 92d Inf Div rec
a parade here at 14
to honor Christopher
and to return his as
City from its hiding*

4.

92nd Division Artillery review, Genoa, Italy.

Occupation and Viareggio Redeployment Area

On 2 May, the 92nd Division reverted from control of 15th Army Group to that of Fifth Army and the IV Corps.

On 4 May, General Von Senger und Etterlin, commanding the XIV Panzer Corps, representing Col. General von Vietinghoff, Commander-in-Chief, Southwest, presented himself to General Clark at his headquarters in Florence to receive his orders for the surrendered armies. The terms of surrender provided for the disarmament and concentration of the German Armies in Italy in certain specified areas under control of the Fifth and Eighth Armies. So far as possible, the Germans were to use their own transportation for movement to their concentration areas and were to be supplied to the maximum extent from their own stocks of rations and materiel. The problem of feeding the captured forces, numbering close to one million, presented a formidable logistical problem.

The 92nd Division was assigned the mission of maintaining order in the Ligurian area, clearing all of the enemy forces from its zone west to the Italian-French border, collecting prisoners of war, and administering to displaced persons. The 442nd Infantry was directed to maintain road blocks and prevent the enemy from infiltrating toward the Italian-French and the Italian-Swiss borders. The 473rd Infantry was directed to maintain road-blocks, prevent enemy infiltration toward the Italian-French border, and maintain contact with French forces along Highway 1.

On 10 May, 365th and 371st Infantry Regiments returned to the 92nd Division. The 365th Infantry, as part of IV Corps on the right of the 92nd Division, was in the Cutigliano sector. The 371st Infantry had taken over much of the Brazilian Expeditionary Force's sector, as it moved to the right and subsequently relieved the Italian Legnano Group in Bologna.

Maj. General Almond debriefs a member of the British #1 Special Force and Partisan Chiefs in Genoa.

The debriefing of Partisan Chiefs continues.

The 442nd and 473rd Infantry Regiments were detached from the 92nd Division. The 365th Infantry took over the duties of the 442nd Infantry, north and west of Genoa. The 371st Infantry assembled in the vicinity of Acqui. The 370th Infantry assumed the duties of the 473rd Infantry in Genoa and west to the French border.

Initially, the 370th Infantry was unable to extend its zone of operation to the French border because the French refused to withdraw. Their occupation of southern Italy was contrary to the Yalta agreement. Reports of the presence of the French in Italy were made to the Commander-in-Chief of the Mediterranean Theater of Operations. He was unable, through his contacts, to have the French withdraw. Eventually, the problem was passed to General Eisenhower who, allegedly, had the French forces under his command. However, he was unable to have them withdraw from Italy. Finally, President Roosevelt overheard someone mention the problem to the Secretary of State. Mr. Roosevelt said, "That is very simple. Cut off their supply of petrol." The next day the French Ambassador's car came to a halt in Rome. Two days later the French withdrew from Italy and the 370th Infantry was able to expand its zone of operations to the French border. In order to provide greater strength in the area, Fifth Army directed that the 34th Division take over, from the 370th Infantry, the area evacuated by the French. This relief was accomplished by 10 July.

At the time the 92nd Division entered Genoa, there were 128 major ships on the bottom of the harbors. Additionally, the harbor was laced with contact and electronic mines. The British Navy was given the mission of clearing the harbor and restoring it to operational capability.

Following the fall of Genoa and immediately after the 92nd Division's reassignment to IV Corps, Lucy Lane Kelley with the IV Corps Red Cross Mobile, arrived in the city. Other members of the Club Mobile were Lydia Sherwood, Susan MacPherson, and Betty Berkley. General Crittenberger had authorized the Club Mobile to go whereever they deemed appropriate. Most of the time they were in the forward area, frequently under hostile fire, dispensing doughnuts (often made with cognac), *Stars & Stripes*, and toilet articles. Although the situation in Genoa was somewhat disorganized, at the time, temporary billets were arranged for the team in the liberated Columbia Hotel.

The capture of Genoa by the 92nd Division produced much of the equipment of the X Flotilla Mas, a PT Boat Flotilla. The X Flotilla Mas was the private Navy of Prince Borghese of Italy. The Borghese Division was his private Army. Both military organizations were raised and paid for by him. Both units fought with the Germans in northern Italy. The Prince received his title from the Church and not from the House of Savoy. Following the surrender of German forces in Italy, Prince Borghese established a reign of

Command inspection of the 769th Tank Destroyer Battalion.

Maj. Gen. Edward M. Almond observes the performance of the 769th Tank Destroyer Battalion.

terror in Northern Italy, hoping to overthrow the monarchy and establish himself as king. He was unsuccessful; however, after a one-month reign by Umberto II, the monarchy was replaced by a democracy.

In rounding up prisoners of war, a number of notorious German and Italian espionage agents, including "Axis Sally," were captured. Also captured was a

The 92nd Division returns the ashes and letters of Christopher Columbus to the city of Genoa in the Piazza della Vittoria Monumento ai Caduti off the Via Brigata Liguria.

92nd Division as an Honor Guard for the return of ashes and letters of Christopher Columbus to the city of Genoa.

copy of General Wolff's final order to his German espionage agents, in northern Italy, directing them to go underground, take civilian jobs, and "stay behind" in northern Italy for the next war or until contacted by some future German government. Partisans had been extremely active through Northern Italy and had, in many cases, set up their own government. The country was filled with ex-soldiers of the Fascist Army which had dissolved. Fascist and Nazi sympathizers still existed and were organized, in part, on the basis of former secret services of the enemy.

The 92nd Division had very little trouble within its area. The chiefs of the five partisan brigades that had been operating in the 92nd Division sector were assembled by General Almond for debriefing and commendation. It was learned, at that time, that three of the brigades were Communist, one was Christian Democrat, and one was made up of escaped felons and crooks. Each chief was presented with a Buffalo Certificate. Officers of the Division and partisans cooperated well in turning over authority to the Allied Military Government within the major cities in the 92nd Division sector. However, in some of the smaller communities where there were no representatives of the Allied Military Government, the former mayors were placed in charge. Thus, inadvertently, Fascist control was temporarily reinstated. In areas where there was little or no United States presence, such as Tourin, the Communists took over. Since that time, Tourin has remained a hotbed of Communist influence.

After the cessation of hostilities, all units of the 92nd Division initiated an intensive rehabilitation program. Each battalion-size unit was subjected to a command inspection by General Almond and his staff. Nightly retreat parades were held at the Piazza della Vittoria in Genoa. Decoration ceremonies for the brave and memorial services for the fallen were conducted.

On 15 May, Lt. Col. Edward L. Rowney left the 92nd Division for an assignment in the War Department. Lt. Col. Thomas St. J. Arnold was relieved as Commanding Officer, 598th Field Artillery Battalion, and again assumed the duties of Assistant Chief of Staff G-3. On 10 May, the 442nd Infantry, with the 77th Anti-Aircraft Brigade attached, was made responsible for Fifth Army's prisoners of war. Subsequently, on 7 June they were relieved of that mission and the 88th Division became Mediterranean Theater of Operation, United States Prisoner of War Command.

On 6 June, the 92nd Division conducted an impressive ceremony in the Piazza della Vittoria in Genoa when it restored the urn containing the mortal remains of Christopher Columbus to its shrine. During the war, the urn containing the ashes of the great discoverer and official documents had been removed from its resting place and taken to the mountains to keep it secure from the hazards of war.

With representation of all elements of the 92nd Division in formation in the Piazza, the horse-drawn caisson, draped with the flag of the City of Genoa,

Maj. General Almond places a wreath under Columbus' ashes after returning them to the City Hall of Genoa.

bearing the urn of Columbus, was escorted through the War Memorial Arch by an honor guard of the 370th Infantry, to the slow cadence of the solemn music played by the 92nd Division Band. A Battery, 598th Field Artillery Battalion, fired an 11-gun salute. Tribute to the memory of Columbus was paid in remarks by General Almond.

The General Staff. AC of S G-3, Lt. Col. Thomas St. J. Arnold; AC of S G-4, Lt. Col. John T. Lorenz; Assistant Division Commander, Brig. Gen. John E. Wood; Commanding Gen., Maj. Gen. Edward M. Almond; Chief of Staff, Col. William McCaffrey; AC of S G-2, Lt. Col. Donald M. MacWillie; AC of S G-1, Lt. Col. Carthal F. Mock, Jr.

Col. William McCaffrey, Chief of Staff, 92nd Division, turned over his duties to Col. Raymond G. Sherman.

Inasmuch as Italy had been a cobelligerent nation, there were no plans to maintain an Army of Occupation anywhere in the country except along the Morgan Line in Venezia Giulia. The Morgan Line had been established by Lt. Gen. Sir William Duthie Morgan, Supreme Allied Commander, Mediterranean Theater of Operations, to separate Allied forces from those of the Yugloslavian Army. It extended from south of Trieste to the Austrian border. Sir William was a direct descendent of the Welsh buccaneer in the Caribbean and Acting Governor of Jamaica. Initially, Allied forces occupying the Morgan Line consisted of the 91st U.S. Division and the 10th Indian Division. Subsequently, this mission was assigned to the 34th U.S. Division and later to the 88th U.S. Division.

In view of the limited requirement for occupation forces, almost all of the American personnel and materiel in Italy were to be shipped out, either to the

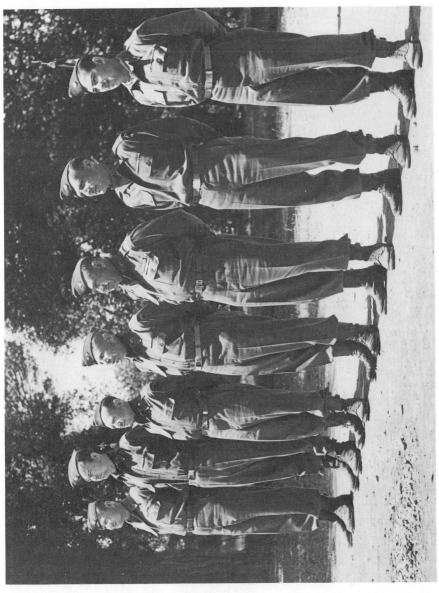

The new General Staff. AC of S G-3, Lt. Col. Thomas St. J. Arnold; AC of S G-4, Lt. Col. John T. Lorenz; Assistant Division Commander, Brig. Gen. John E. Wood; C. G Maj. Gen. Edward M. Almond; C/S Col. Raymond G. Sherman, AC of S, Lt. Col. Donald M. MacWillie; AC of S, Lt. Col. Carthal F. Mock, Jr.

Maj. Gen. Edward M. Almond bids farewell to the 92nd Division.

Pacific or the United States. This entailed separating out some individuals for eventual discharge and reorganization and training of units for redeployments in accordance with directives of the War Department. To accomplish this task, Fifth Army established six redeployment and training centers. One such area

Lt. Col. Thomas St. John Arnold, GSC, Assistant Chief of Staff G-3, 92nd Infantry Division, and Chief of Staff of the Viareggio Redeployment Center, Italy, 1944.

Lt. Colonel Arnold, Assistant Chief of Staff G-3 (center, front row) together with his officers and enlisted men of the G-3 section.

Cross of Merit in War presented to Lt. Colonel Arnold by Prince Umberto, Lt. General of the Realm, later King Umberto II of Italy.

The colors of the 92nd Division are decorated with the Italian Military Cross by His Royal Highness, Prince Umberto, Lt. General of the Realm, later King Umberto II of Italy.

The 92nd Division honors its fallen comrades in an impressive Memorial Day Ceremony.

American cemetery in northern Italy, 92nd Division Memorial Services.

After being killed by Partisans in the Italian Alps, Mussolini and his mistress were hung upside down in a service station in Milan.

was the Viareggio Redeployment Training Center located in a pine forest south of Viareggio on property belonging to the Duke of Solviette. Maj. Gen. Edward M. Almond was placed in command of this area with Lt. Col. Thomas St. J. Arnold as Chief of Staff. The 92nd Division was assigned to the Viareggio Redeployment Center.

During the period 10 to 17 June, the 92nd Division moved from the Genoa area to the Viareggio Redeployment Training Center. During the final days of combat the Division had captured great quantities of wine and cognac. As it moved into the Training Center this was placed under Division control, and a barrel of cognac was placed at the end of each company and battery street so that anyone could fill his canteen or bottle with cognac at any time, day or night. Surprisingly, intoxication was a rare offense.

An intensive training program was initiated by the Division to prepare all troops for redeployment. On 30 June, Brig. Gen. William H. Colbern, Commanding General, 92nd Division Artillery, and Col. William J. McCaffery, departed for assignments within the United States. Col. Raymond G. Sherman, who had commanded the 370th Infantry, assumed the duties of Chief of Staff.

On 5 July, Headquarters, 15th Army Group, was dissolved at Verona, Italy. Its American contingent became the nucleus of Headquarters, United States Forces in Austria. On 15 August Maj. Gen. Edward M. Almond left Italy to assume command of the 2nd Division in Texas. Brig. Gen. John E. Wood, the Assistant Division Commander, assumed command of the Division. Col. Raymond G. Sherman was designated Assistant Division Commander. Col. Donald Dunford was appointed Chief of Staff.

On 2 October, Colonel Dunford and Lt. Colonel Arnold left the Division for assignments with the 88th Division on the Morgan Line. Colonel Dunford became the Division Artillery Commander, 88th Division, and Lt. Colonel Arnold assumed command of the 337th Field Artillery Battalion. Lt. Colonel Osborn became the Chief of Staff, 92nd Division, and Lt. Colonel Lane was appointed Assistant Chief of Staff, G-3.

On 19 October, His Royal Highness, Prince Umberto, Lieutenant General of the Realm, subsequently King Umberto II of Italy, awarded the Cross of Merit in War to the 92nd Division and awarded similar decorations to 38 officers and enlisted men of the Division. On 16 November, the 92nd Division departed for the United States, and on 28 November, the 92nd Division was inactivated at Camp Kilmer, New Jersey.

Maj. General Almond awards Buffalo Certificates to Partisan Chieftains, Genoa, Italy, 1945.

NOTES

Introduction
Pages 1-8
1. Herbert O. Yardley, *The American Black Chamber*, p. xii, Ballantine Books, New York.

The Situation
Pages 9-14
2. Subsequently, Col. Thomas St. J. Arnold served under his command in NATO forces in Germany for 1½ years in 1960-1962.

Piercing the Gothic Line
Pages 29-33
3. The hero of Gordon Glasco's novel *The Days of Eternity* was a German officer, Military Governor of the town of Montefalco, north of the area. The reference in the novel to "the Americans coming from Pistoia," "the far off explosions coming faster," and "shimmering flashes of deep orange light" coincides with the advance of the 3rd Battalion, 370th Infantry, supported by the 598th Field Artillery Battalion. Further, the hero's decision to desert, in order to escape execution, coincides with the 3rd Battalion's capture of the first officer prisoner of war taken by the 370th Infantry. Also, about that time, the 3rd Battalion lost a 12-month patrol. It was cut off by the Germans. Subsequently, a German prisoner of war stated that in the darkness they would not have known that the patrol was not friendly if it had not attempted to challenge in English.

The 92nd Division on the Offensive
Pages 43-64
4. 1st Lt. Edward Brooks, 366th Infantry, married an Italian young woman and became the first black United States Senator, from Massachusetts.

The February Offensive
Pages 89-112
5. After retiring from the Army in the grade of Lieutenant General, Rowney became Chief Arms Control and Disarmament negotiator with the rank of Ambassador.

15th Army Group Spring Offensive
Pages 151-167
6. Daniel K. Inouye in 1959 was elected to the U.S. House of Representatives as Hawaii's first Congressman and later, in 1962, was elected to the U.S. Senate.

Appendix A

ACTIVATION AND TRAINING

The 92nd Infantry Division was activated on 15 October 1942, at four widely-separated military installations: Division Headquarters and Headquarters Company, Headquarters Special Troops, Military Police Platoon, 792nd Ordnance Company, 92nd Quartermaster Company, 92nd Signal Company, 92nd Cavalry Reconnaissance Troop, Headquarters and Headquarters Battery, 92nd Division Artillery, and the 600th Field Artillery Battalion at Fort McClellan, Alabama; the 365th Infantry and the 597th Field Artillery Battalion at Camp Attenbury, Indiana; the 370th Infantry and 598th Field Artillery Battalion at Camp Breckenridge, Kentucky; and the 371st Infantry and 599th Field Artillery Battalion at Camp Robinson, Arkansas.

Maj. Gen. Edward M. Almond was designated Division Commander. Brig. Gen. John E. Wood was designated Assistant Division Commander. Brig. Gen. William H. Colbern was assigned as Division Artillery Commander, and Col. Frank E. Barber was appointed Chief of Staff. Colonel Barber was killed by artillery fire three days after he arrived in Italy. A cadre of 128 officers and 1,200 enlisted men, selected from the 93rd Infantry Division (Black) was used to form the 92nd Infantry Division.

Officers and enlisted men began to arrive shortly thereafter. By the end of November 1942, the Division had received most of its fillers and reached a strength of approximately 15,000. Shortly thereafter the Division was brought to an over-strength position of approximately 7 percent officers and 15 percent enlisted men.

The prescribed Individual Training Program (ITP) was initiated by all elements of the Division on 1 November 1942. Following the completion of this phase of training on 15 April 1943, the Division Artillery, *i.e.*, Headquarters and Headquarters Battery, 92nd Division Artillery, 597th, 598th, 599th, and 600th Field Artillery Battalion were assembled at Camp Robinson, Arkansas, under the command of Brig. Gen. William H. Colbern, for implementation of the Unit Training Program (UTP). Other elements of the Division were assembled in late April 1943, at Fort Huachuca, Arizona, for unit training. The Division Artillery moved from Camp Robinson, Arkansas, and joined the remainder of the Division at Fort Huachuca, Arizona, on 10 May 1943. The 92nd Infantry Division completed its Unit Training phase on 15 August 1943.

The Combined Training Program (CTP) began on 16 August and lasted until 15

Col. Frank E. Barber, Chief of Staff. Activation of the 92nd Infantry Division, 15 October 1945, Fort McClellan, Alabama, killed on his third day in Italy.

January 1944. This phase of training was followed by Division Exercises which were conducted during the period 3 December 1943-15 January 1944. This was followed by a series of tests.

In January 1944 the Division moved to Merryville, Louisiana, and participated with the 44th and 75th Infantry Divisions and the 8th Armored Division in the Sixth Louisiana Maneuvers. Following the maneuvers, the Division was deemed adequately trained and ready for combat. The Division returned to Fort Huachuca, Arizona, and prepared for an overseas assignment.

Colonel Raymond Sherman's 370th Regimental Combat Team, consisting of the following, was selected to precede the Division overseas:

370th Field Artillery Battalion
598th Field Artillery Battalion
B Company, 317th Engineer (C) Battalion
B Company, plus 1 Platoon, D Company, 317th Medical Battalion
Detachment, 92nd Quartermaster Company
Detachment, 92nd Signal Company
Detachment, 92nd Military Police Platoon
Detachment, 792nd Ordnance (LM) Company

Beginning on 4 April 1944, the Combat Team replaced its poorest-trained men and intensified its training in anticipation of its departure.

The Combat Team staged at Camp Patrick Henry, Virginia, and sailed from Hampton Roads on 15 July 1944 for North Africa, aboard the luxury liner, S.S. *Mariposa*. It trans-shipped at the port of Oran in North Africa, aboard a U.S. Navy transport and landed in Naples, Italy, on 1 August 1944. On arrival in Italy, the 370th Regimental Combat Team was moved into the crater of an inactive volcano, just north of Naples, which had been the King's hunting preserve. The next ten days were spent in assembly of equipment, orientation, and physical conditioning. For battle indoctrination, small groups of officers and enlisted men were assigned to Armored Infantry and Artillery Battalions of the 1st Armored Division.

The Combat Team was inspected by Maj. Gen. Jacob Devers in its bivouac area on 10 August 1944 and commenced its move by rail (40/8 boxcars) to its staging area in Civitivecchia, Italy. On 22 August, it moved to the vicinity of Bagni di Cascione and prepared for entry into the line.

When the 3rd Battalion, 370th Infantry Regiment, moved into the line near Pontedera, Italy, relieving the 14th Armored Infantry Battalion- and the 598th Field Artillery Battalion-occupied positions in the vicinity on the night of 23 August 1944, the first units of the 92nd Infantry Division had gone into combat.

Brig. Gen. John E. Wood, the Assistant Division Commander, with an advance party of an aide and one officer from each of the General Staff sections, flew to Italy in August 1944. The Division advanced detachment followed a short time later. The remainder of the Division left the United States in successive stages during the month of September 1944.

A total of 94 weeks had been devoted to organization and training of the 92nd Infantry Division. A total of 87.9 percent of its personnel had qualified with their individual weapons.

Maj. Gen. Edward M. Almond, Commanding General, 92nd Infantry Division.

Brig. Gen. John E. Wood, Assistant Division Commander, Maj. Gen. Edward M. Almond, Division Commander, and Brig. Gen. William H. Colbern, Division Artillery Commander.

Training at Camp Breckenridge, Kentucky. Infantrymen learning to manhandle an antitank piece into action.

Training at Fort Huachuca, Arizona — a light tank accompanying an infantry patrol.

Appendix B

92ND INFANTRY DIVISION AND ATTACHMENTS

92nd Infantry Division

Headquarters and Headquarters Company
92nd Cavalry Reconnaissance Troop, Mechanized
365th Infantry Regiment
370th Infantry Regiment
371st Infantry Regiment
92nd Division Artillery, Headquarters and Headquarters Battery
    597th Field Artillery Battalion (105-mm Howitzer)
    598th Field Artillery Battalion (105-mm Howitzer)
    599th Field Artillery Battalion (105-mm Howitzer)
    600th Field Artillery Battalion (155-mm Howitzer)
317th Engineer Combat Battalion
Headquarters Special Troops
    92nd Signal Company
    92nd Quartermaster Company
    92nd Ordnance Light Maintenance Company
    Military Police Platoon
    92nd Infantry Division Band
317th Medical Battalion

Attachments
United States Units

Infantry
    366th Infantry Regiment
    442nd Infantry Regiment
    473rd Infantry Regiment

135th Infantry Regiment (34th Infantry Division)
337th Infantry Regiment (85th Infantry Division)
Armored
2nd Armored Group, Headquarters and Headquarters Company
751st Tank Battalion (Medium)
755th Tank Battalion (Medium)
758th Tank Battalion (Light)
760th Tank Battalion (Less Companies A and D)
Field Artillery
424th Field Artillery Group, Headquarters and Headquarters Battery
428th Field Artillery Group, Headquarters and Headquarters Battery
75th Field Artillery Battalion (155-mm Howitzer)
329th Field Artillery Battalion (105-mm Howitzer) (85th Infantry Division)
530th Field Artillery Battalion (155-mm Gun) (Less Battery A)
766th Field Artillery Battalion
1125th Armored Field Artillery Battalion (105-mm Howitzer)
Antiaircraft
45th Anti-aircraft Artillery Brigade, Headquarters and Headquarters Battery
434th Anti-aircraft Artillery Battalion (Automatic Weapons) (Self-Propelled)
435th Anti-aircraft Artillery Battalion (Automatic Weapons) (Semi-Mobile)
Battery C, 351st Anti-aircraft Artillery Battalion (Searchlight)
Tank Destroyer
894th Tank Destroyer Battalion
701st Tank Destroyer Battalion
769th Tank Destroyer Battalion
Chemical
84th Chemical Mortar Battalion
179th Chemical Smoke Generating Company
Engineer
232nd Engineer Combat Company
Medical
15th Field Hospital (Unit B)
673rd Collecting Company
Quartermaster
43rd QM War Dog Platoon
Signal
Two Pigeon Lofts
Adjutant General Corps
37th Special Service Company
206th AGF Band
British Units
Field Artillery
10th Army Group, Royal Artillery (AGRA)
17th Medium Regiment, Royal Artillery
111th Army Field Regiment, Royal Artillery (Less One)
Detachment, 5th Battery, 8th Survey Regiment, Royal Artillery

Antiaircraft Artillery
   62nd Anti-Aircraft Brigade
   26th Light Anti-Aircraft Regiment
   47th Light Anti-Aircraft Regiment
   56th Light Anti-Aircraft Regiment
   71st Heavy Anti-Aircraft Regiment (Less 299th Battery)
   76th Heavy Anti-Aircraft Regiment
   53rd Anti-Aircraft Operations Room

Italian Units

23rd Engineer Battalion (2 Companies)
Mule Pack Battalion (Provisional)

Appendix C

HOSTILE FORCES OPPOSING THE 92ND DIVISION IN ITALY

Hostile forces in contact with the 92nd Division in its zone of operations were approximately the same strength as those of the friendly forces. Even the main effort of the 92nd Division never had preponderance in strength except a slight advantage at the critical point. Any shortage in numbers in the hostile units were more than offset by the rugged terrain selected for the defense by the enemy, his well prepared positions, and his coastal defense guns at Punta Bianca.

Hostile forces opposing the 92nd Division during its operations in Northern Italy were elements of the following four groups:

German Command South-West and Army Group C
    Field Marshal Albert Kesselring, initially, C-in-C
    General Vietinghoff, subsequently, C-in C
Fourteenth Army
    Lieutenant General Lemelsen, Commanding
LI Mountain Corps
    Major General Haack, Commanding
LXXV Infantry Corps
    Major General Schlemner, Commanding

Elements of the LI Mountain Corps and approximate dates of contact are as follows:
65th Grenadier Division   23 August-4 October 1944
    Major General Pfeiffer, Commanding
42nd Jaeger Division   5 October-24 October 1944
    Major General Jost, Commanding
1st Parachute Division   28 September-30 September 1944
    Brigadier General Schulz, Commanding
148th Grenadier Division   23 October 1944-24 April 1945
    Brigadier General Fretter-Pico, Commanding

San Marco (Maine) Division (Italian)   28 October 1944-24 April 1945
    General Farina, Commanding
Monte Rosa (Alpini) Division   28 October 1944-24 April 1945
    General Mainardi, Commanding
Italia (Bersiglieri) Division   28 October 1944-24 April 1945
    General Carloni, Commanding
101st Cavalry Reconnaissance Battalion   28 October 1944-24 April 1945
4th Mountain Battalion   26 December 1944-28 February 1945
Mittenwald (Mountain) Battalion   26 December 1944-28 February 1945
148th Fusilier Battalion   8 February-24 April 1945
Kesselring Machine Gun Battalion   8 February-24 April 1945
361st Panzer Grenadier Regiment   10 April-24 April 1945
    (90th Panzer Grenadier Division,
        Colonel Hans F. Wunderlich, Commanding)
135th Fortress Brigade   18 April-24 April

Elements of the LXXV Infantry Corps and approximate dates of contact are as
follows:

34th Infantry Division   25 April-2 May 1945
    Major General Lieb, Commanding
5th Mountain Division   28 April-2 May 1945
    Colonel Steets, Commanding

Appendix D

COMMENTS BY GERMAN PERSONNEL OPPOSING THE 92ND DIVISION

The following comments by Germans, who had opposed the 92nd Infantry Division, were obtained in interviews and through questioning by Lt. Col. Thomas St. J. Arnold after the end of hostilities in Italy.

A 1st Lieutenant of Infantry, 1st Parachute Division, at a prisoner of war enclosure, Leghorn, Italy, September 1945:

> I was a company commander in the 1st Parachute Division. In September 1944 we were withdrawing from north of Montignoso in the vicinity of Prunetta when the negro troops moved into that area. Your advance was too rapid. I saw you come forward in trucks, dismount, and advance. I requested artillery but our artillery ammunition was so low that strict orders had been issued to fire only in the event of a determined attack. That night as we continued the withdrawal I lost contact with the company on my right which was a part of another regiment. You sent out a 12-man patrol that moved into the gap. Personnel of my company thought it was the company on our right and paid no attention to it for some time. However, later some of my men challenged and your patrol answered with fire. We knew immediately that they were American personnel. I stopped the withdrawal of my company, closed the gap, and captured all 12 of your men. Had they not answered by fire we would probably not have paid any attention to them. You would then have been able to move in a sufficient force to cut off the withdrawal of my company.

A Captain, 101st Cavalry Reconnaissance Battalion, at a prisoner of war enclosure, Leghorn, Italy, September 1945:

> The 101st Cavalry Reconnaissance Battalion was attached to the 148th

Infantry Division for observation duty as directed by the Division G-2. Your massed fire from very heavy machine guns ["Infantry weapons shoot": This was a mass concentration of fire from all of the infrequently-used weapons of the division on targets selected by the division G-3. These concentrations were of five minutes duration and in general were fired every half hour. They included .50 cal MG, 37-mm Tank Guns, 40-mm Antiaircraft Guns, and 57-mm Antitank Guns] was terrific. They were not only casualty-producing but very demoralizing. This tended to restrict movements in the forward areas and in some cases caused us to withdraw from some of our most forward blocking positions.

I was at an observation post on 8 February 1945 when you launched your attack. It seemed to get off to a good start, particularly in the coastal area. Early in the afternoon of this first day, our troops were preparing to withdraw to positions to the rear when apparently the drive of your attack began to weaken. As a result of this, it was decided to try to hold in present positions which our troops were eventually able to do.

A Staff Sergeant, Transportation Company, 90th Panzer Grenadier Division at a prisoner of war enclosure, Leghorn, Italy, September 1945:

I was a section leader in the truck battalion of the 90th Panzer Division. On or about 11 April 1944 we transported infantry troops of our division from its reserve position to the 148th Infantry Division area. Airplanes attacked us in the Cisa Pass but we came through all right.

Brig. Gen. Otto Fretter-Pico, Commanding General, 148th Infantry Division, Munich, Germany, November 1948-February 1949:

I considered the 92nd Division's combat capabilities good. I believed, however, they showed a noticeable lack of combat experience. Had they been more aggressive they would have achieved their goal much sooner.

My principal worry, prior to the April attack, was the possibility of an attack from the sea. Such an action would have made my position untenable.

Your ships off the Ligurian Coast during the April attack had the effect of constantly reminding me of the possibility of such an attack. The naval gunfire from those ships was ineffectual.

The attack of partisans on 16 November 1944, in an attempt to secure Sassi and Eglio from the rear, was apparently ineffectual in that it was never brought to my attention. However, the partisans were a continuous source of trouble to me. They harassed me in the rear areas and along my supply lines so that I constantly had to divert combat troops from the front to protect those supply lines and my rear installations.

I feel certain that the supplies which you dropped from airplanes to the partisans just prior to 16 November 1944 were received by them since none of those supplies fell into our hands.

CRITIQUE *after* BATTLE

BRIG.GEN. FRETTER PICO
148TH GERMAN DIVISION

LT. COL. THOMAS ST. JOHN ARNOLD
92ND U S DIVISION

NOVEMBER 1948 – FEBRUARY 1949
MUNICH, GERMANY

The attack of the 285th Infantry on Vergemoli on 4 December 1944 was a diversionary attack for the effort that was to follow on the left at a later date.

The weaknesses of your deployment in the Serchio Valley at the time of my attack on 26 December 1944 were that your troops were deployed on a front which was too long for the number of men available and your reserves were too far in the rear areas which prevented their being deployed immediately.

I stopped my attack in the vicinity of Fornaci because I did not have a sufficient force to allow me to push on to Bagni di Lucca or Lucca. The objective of my attack was to stop the American attack on Bologna by diverting reserves from that effort. This objective was accomplished.

My initial reaction to the attack of the 92nd Division on 8 to 11 February 1945 was that of not too much concern as I knew that the 92nd Division had not received front line replacements for this attack. I did not consider this action as a major offense, but only as an attack to relieve the fight at the main front. I was right in that the attack was halted and no other attacks followed immediately.

My plan of withdrawal was to first withdraw to the "green" line from La Spezia to Carrara and then from one defense line to another across the Cisa Pass into the Po Valley. A plan of withdrawal was not undertaken at the time of your attack on 8 to 11 February 1945. I would have done so if your attacks had continued.

With the approach of spring, I knew that my position south of the Apennines was untenable. Consequently, I made repeated requests for permission to withdraw to positions in the Cisa Pass. My higher headquarters reasoned that if I withdrew, the entire coast to Genoa would be open to you. So, in spite of the broad front I was holding, I was ordered to defend it at all costs. I do not think this was a good decision. It appeared to be such a waste of men and material when the ultimate results were so obvious.

The emplacement for the coastal guns at Punta Bianca was extremely well constructed. We were able to continue delivery of fire in spite of dive bombers, medium and heavy bombardment, and artillery fire. Of the three different types of attacks, heavy bombardment had the most effect. This was due to the tremendous concussion and shock. In spite of this, however, these guns were able to stay in action until you were in a position to outflank them.

The loudspeaker broadcasts and other propaganda efforts made by your Psychological Warfare Branch in the coastal area had little or no effect on Germans but had a marked effect on Poles and personnel of other nationalities. The newspaper, *Front Post*, fired by you in artillery shells was of particular interest to me as well as other officers of my command for it provided us with the news we were unable to get from our own sources.

Initially, we were misled by the dummy armored division which you moved up the Serchio Valley from Bagni di Lucca to Barga on the nights of the 3rd and 4th of April 1945. I delayed moving reserve units from the Serchio Valley to the coastal area for two days, while waiting to see if an attack would be launched from that area. The lack of fire from high velocity weapons led us to believe that there was no appreciable concentration of armor in the area.

A regimental combat team, complete with artillery and other supporting elements of the 90th Panzer Grenadier Division was ordered to reinforce the 148th Division on the west coast of Italy in April 1945. However, your Air Force attacked this regimental combat team while it was enroute and only one infantry battalion was able to get through the Cisa Pass. The remainder of this combat team, including its artillery was turned around and used elsewhere on the front.

The naval personnel from the port of La Spezia who the 148th Division attempted to employ as reinforcements in April of 1945 were completely ineffectual.

Hans Roettiger, Chief of Staff, Army Group G, Frankfurt, Germany, April 1940:

The attack in the Serchio Valley on 26 December 1944 was meant only as a reconnaissance in force. This attack had been planned as one with limited objective. The aim was to get our own forces back to their line of departure. A more extensive attack into the depth of the enemy front (perhaps up to Lucca) would have necessitated a much larger force than was at the disposal of the High Command of Army Group G.

The artillery bombardment on the coastal guns at Punta Bianca had only an effect of limited duration. This coastal artillery had a large share in the active defense against the attacks of 92nd Infantry on the coastal line.

The propagandistic effect of the loudspeaker broadcasts by the Psychological Warfare Branch on the German Troops was practically nil.

The temporary reinforcement of the 148th German Division by the 90th Panzer Grenadier Division seemed necessary in order to prevent an early break-through of American forces on La Spezia. The extent of this reinforcement was, as far as I can remember, the strength of a reinforced infantry regiment.

Appendix E

15TH ARMY GROUP TROOP LIST, APRIL 1945

15TH ARMY GROUP
Gen. Mark W. Clark, Commanding

15TH ARMY GROUP TROOPS
8th Anti-Aircraft Brigade
  Brig. C. A. Fenton, Commanding
    62nd Heavy Anti-Aircraft Regiment
    22nd Light Anti-Aircraft Regiment
    31st Light Anti-Aircraft Regiment
      (less two batteries)
    568th Searchlight Battery
      (less one troop)
    48th Anti-Aircraft Operations Room
66th Anti-Aircraft Brigade,
(Administration Fifth Army)
  Brig. T. S. Smith, OBE, TD, Commanding
    59th Heavy Anti-Aircraft Regiment
    12th Light Anti-Aircraft Regiment
    13th Light Anti-Aircraft Regiment
    29th Light Anti-Aircraft Regiment
    535th Seachlight Battery
      (less one section)
    52nd Anti-Aircraft Operations Room
    55th Anti-Aircraft Operations Room
Number 1 Field Radar Operations Group
    54th Anti-Aircraft Operations Room

FIFTH ARMY
Lt. Gen. Lucian K. Truscott, Jr.,
Commanding

FIFTH ARMY TROOPS
Fifth Army Artillery
  Brig. Gen. Guy O. Kurtz, Artillery Officer

    630th Automatic Weapons Battalion
Fifth Army Engineer Headquarters
  Brig. Gen. Frank O. Bowman, Chief
    Engineer
    1338th Engineer Combat Group
      Col. David F. Shaw, Commanding
    169th Engineer Combat Battalion
    182nd Engineer Combat Battalion
    185th Engineer Combat Battalion
    1168th Engineer Combat Group
      Col. S. A. Armogida, Commanding
    92nd Engineer General Service
      Regiment
      Col. George W. Bennett,
      Commanding
    175th Engineer General Service
      Regiment
      Lt. Col. Alexander H. Miller,
      Commanding
    224th Engineer General Service
      Regiment
      Lt. Col. Otto J. Rhode, Commanding
    226th Engineer General Service
      Regiment
      Lt. Col. Alanzo Ferguson,
      Commanding
    1554th Engineer Heavy Pontoon
      Battalion

85TH INFANTRY DIVISION
Maj. Gen. John B. Coulter, Commanding

92ND INFANTRY DIVISION
Maj. Gen. E. M. Almond, Commanding

II CORPS
Maj. Gen. Geoffrey M. Keyes, Commanding

II CORPS TROOPS
II Corps Artillery
  Brig. Gen. Henry D. Jay, Artillery Officer
    15th Observation Battalion
    178th Field Artillery Group
    Col. Ansel B. Godfrey, Commanding
      248th Field Artillery Battalion
      527th Field Artillery Battalion
      765th Field Artillery Battalion
      12th Battery, 54th Super Heavy
        Regiment (Br.)
      "A" Battery, 530th Field Artillery
        Battalion
    77th Field Artillery Group
    Lt. Col. Harold S. Isaacson,
    Commanding
      173rd Field Artillery Battalion
      631st Field Artillery Battalion
      936th Field Artillery Battalion
    423rd Field Artillery Group
    Col. James H. Workman, Commanding
      178th Field Artillery Battalion
      536th Field Artillery Battalion
      985th Field Artillery Battalion
      11th Battery, 54th Super Heavy
        Regiment (Br.)
    71st Anti-Aircraft Brigade
    Brig. Gen. R. R. Hendrix, Commanding
      209th Anti-Aircraft Group
      Col. Kenneth C. Townson,
      Commanding
        401st Gun Battalion
        403rd Gun Battalion
        105th Automatic Weapons
          Battalion (Self-Propelled)
        432nd Automatic Weapons Battalions
          (Self-Propelled)
      "B" Battery, 360th Searchlight Battalion
II Corps Engineers
  Col. Joseph O. Killian, Chief Engineer
    19th Engineer Combat Group
    Col. John De Cole, Jr., Commanding
      401st Engineer Combat Battalion
      402nd Engineer Combat Battalion
    39th Engineer Combat Group
    Col. Thomas C. Green, Commanding
      404th Engineer Combat Battalion
      643rd Engineer Combat Battalion
    1755th Engineer Treadway Bridge
      Company
    752nd Tank Battalion

757th Tank Battalion
804th Tank Destroyer Battalion
805th Tank Destroyer Battalion
91st Cavalry Reconnaissance Squadron

34TH INFANTRY DIVISION
Maj. Gen. Charles L. Bolte, Commanding

88TH INFANTRY DIVISION
Maj. Gen. Paul W. Kendall, Commanding

91ST INFANTRY DIVISION
Maj. Gen. William G. Livesay, Commanding
  91st Division Artillery

6TH SOUTH AFRICAN
ARMORED DIVISION
Maj. Gen. W. H. E. Poole, CB, DSO,
Commanding

LEGNANO COMBAT GROUP (Italian)
Maj. Gen. Umberto Utili, Commanding

IV CORPS
Maj. Gen. W. D. Crittenberger, Commanding

IV CORPS TROOPS
IV Corps Artillery
  Brig. Gen. W. C. Crane, Artillery Officer
    7th Army Group Royal Artillery
    Brig. R. Morley, MC, Commanding
      178th Medium Regiment (5.5-inch)
      2nd Medium Regiment (4.5-inch
      253rd Battery, 17th Medium
        Regiment (5.5-inch)
      8th Survey Regiment (less 56th
        Battery and one troop)
      26th Light Anti-Aircraft
        Regiment
      53rd Anti-Aircraft Operations
        Room
    424th Field Artillery Group
      Col. Wellington A. Samouce,
      Commanding
    633rd Field Artillery Battalion
    403rd Field Artillery Battalion
    328th Field Artillery Battalion
    910th Field Artillery Battalion
    360th Searchlight Battalion, "C"
      Battery
IV Corps Engineers
  Col. Douglas H. Gillete, Chief Engineer
    1108th Engineer Combat Group
    Col. John O. Colonna, Commanding

235th Engineer Combat Battalion
255th Engineer Combat Battalion
337th Engineer Combat Battalion
23rd Italian Engineer Combat
Battalion
1029th Engineer Treadway Bridge
Company
751st Tank Battalion
760th Tank Battalion
679th Tank Destroyer Battalion
701st Tank Destroyer Battalion
894th Tank Destroyer Battalion

1ST ARMORED DIVISION
Maj. Gen. Vernon E. Prichard, Commanding

10TH MOUNTAIN INFANTRY DIVISION
Maj. Gen. G. P. Hays, Commanding

1ST INFANTRY DIVISION,
Brazilian Expeditionary Force
Maj. Gen. Joao Batista Mascarenhas de
Moraes, Commanding

EIGHTH ARMY
Lt. Gen. Sir R. L. McCreery KCB, DSO,
MBE, MC, Commanding

EIGHTH ARMY TROOPS
Royal Artillery
Brig. F. S. Siggers, CBE, MC, Artillery
Officer
"A" Field Radar Regiment
8th Survey Regiment (one troop)
2nd Calibration Troop
"A" Special Calibration Section
12th Anti-Aircraft Brigade
Brig. G. A. Eastwood, DSO, OBE,
Commanding
8th Polish Heavy Anti-Aircraft
Regiment (less one battery)
55th Heavy Anti-Aircraft Regiment
(less one battery)
57th Heavy Anti-Aircraft Regiment
(one battery)
7th Polish Light Anti-Aircraft Regiment
14th Light Anti-Aircraft Regiment
30th Light Anti-Aircraft Regiment
53rd Light Anti-Aircraft Regiment
(one battery)
3rd Carpathian Light Anti-Aircraft
Regiment (one battery)

5th Kresowa Light Anti-Aircraft
Regiment (one battery)
7th Italian Light Anti-Aircraft Regiment
(23rd battery)
49th Anti-Aircraft Operations Room
831st Italian Searchlight Platoon
Royal Engineers
Brig. B. C. Davey, CBE, Chief Engineer
25th Armored Engineer Brigade
Brig. E. W. H. Clarke, DSO, Commanding
51st Royal Tank Regiment
1st Armored Engineer Regiment
(under command V Corps)
2nd Armored Engineer Regiment
170th Chief Engineer Works
Col. N. Wilson, Commanding
1st Canadian Drilling Company
82nd Workshop and Park Company
(less four advance park sections)
16th Army Group Royal Engineer
Col. C. J. Strainer, Commanding
25th Road Construction Company
South African Engineer Corps
173rd Army Field Park Company
21st General Headquarters Troops
228th Field Company
562nd Field Company
579th Field Company
1210th General Headquarters
Troops
102nd Field Company
107th Field Company
754th Field Company
466th Indian Corps Troops Indian
Engineers
1st Field Company
14th Field Company
97th Field Company
301st Corps Field Park Company
20th Army Group Royal Engineers
(Airfields)
Col. W. W. Brown, OBE,
Commanding
14th Airfield Construction Group
15th Airfield Construction Group
69th Airfield Construction Group
24th Army Group Royal Engineers
Col. H. C. W. Eking, Commanding
Commander Royal Engineer Roads
South African Engineer Corps
21st Field Company South African
Engineer Corps
27th Road Construction Company
Royal Engineers

803rd Road Construction Company
  Royal Engineers
857th Quarrying Company Royal
  Engineers
156th Commander Royal Engineer
Works
  567th Army Troops Company
  288th Works Section
  291st Works Section
  171st Tunneling Company
  738th Army Troops Company
    (Palestinian)
  1st Camouflage Company
    (Palestinian)
  41st Harbor Construction Company
    South African Engineer Corps
    (less one section)
  Headquarters Oil Storage and
    Pipeline Construction Group
  723rd Artisan Works Company
  1st Pipeline Operation and
    Maintenance Unit
  2nd Pipeline Operation and
    Maintenance Unit
  863rd Mechanical Equipment
    Company
  139th Mechanical Equipment
    Company
2nd Independent Parachute Brigade Group
Brig. C. H. B. Pritchard, DSO,
Commanding
  Royal Artillery
    64th Air Landing Light Battery
    300th Air Landing Anti-Tank Battery
    3rd Forward Observation Unit
  Royal Engineers
    2nd Parachute Squadron
    4th Parachute Squadron
    5th Parachute Battalion
    6th Parachute Battalion
    1st Independent Parachute Platoon
  86th (Army) Area
  12th Royal Lancer (Prince of Wales')
  7th Queen's Own Hussars
  1st Armored Delivery Regiment
  200th Armored Delivery Regiment
  1st Special Demolition Squadron
    (Popski's Private Army)
  10th Battalion The Rifle Brigade
  "F" Reconnaissance Squadron (Italian)

6TH BRITISH ARMORED DIVISION
Maj. Gen. H. Murray, DSO, Commanding

V CORPS
Lt. Gen. C. F. Keightley, CB, CBE, DSO,
Commanding

V CORPS TROOPS
Royal Artillery
  Brig. E. B. de Fonblanque, DSO, Artillery
  Officer
    54th Super Heavy Regiment (less two
      batteries)
    5th Survey Regiment
    57th Heavy Anti-Aircraft Regiment
      (less one battery)
    52nd Light Anti-Aircraft Regiment
    651st Air OP Squadron
    654th Air OP Squadron
    323rd Searchlight Battery
    17th Field Regiment (one battery)
    57th Anti-Tank Regiment (one battery)
    55th Heavy Anti-Aircraft Regiment
      (one battery)
1st Army Group Royal Artillery
  Brig. H. A. Maconochie, Commanding
    4th Medium Regiment (5.5-inch)
      (less one section)
    26th Medium Regiment (4.5-inch)
      (less one troop)
    58th Medium Regiment (5.5-inch)
    70th Medium Regiment (4.5-inch)
    80th Medium Regiment (5.5-inch)
    75th Heavy Regiment (Mixed)
    125th Meteorological Section
2nd Army Group Royal Artillery
  Brig F. H. C. Rogers, CBE, MC,
  Commanding
    5th Medium Regiment (5.5-inch)
    73rd Medium Regiment (4.5-inch)
    74th Medium Regiment (5.5-inch)
    76th Medium Regiment (4.5-inch)
    102nd Medium Regiment (5.5-inch)
    61st Heavy Regiment (Mixed)
    127th Meteorological Section
Royal Engineers
  Brig. J. V. C. Moberley, CBE, Chief
  Engineer
    5th Corps Troops Royal Engineers
      42nd Field Company
      564th Field Company
      565th Field Company
      751st Field Company
      215th Corps Field Park Company
      22nd Mechanical Equipment Platoon
      586th Army Field Company
      85th Company South African

Engineer Corps (camouflage)
(detachment)
22nd Army Group Royal Engineers
Headquarters Eighth Army Troops Royal
Engineers
561st Army Field Company
587th Army Field Company
585th Corps Field Park Company
Headquarters South African Corps Troops
South African Engineer Corps
1st Field Company
11th Field Company
13th Field Company
22nd Field Company
31st Road Construction Company
1st Armored Engineer Regiment
(ex-25th Armored Engineer Brigade)
3rd Field Regiment
52nd Field Regiment
53rd Field Regiment
64th Field Regiment
24th Field Regiment (Self-Propelled)
4th Mahratta Anti-Tank Regiment
Indian Engineers
7th Field Company
66th Field Company
69th Field Company
47th Field Park Company
5th Royal Mahrattas Machine Gun Battalion
6th DCO Lancers (Watson's Horse)
1st Jaipur Infantry Battalion (Indian State
Force)
21st Tank Brigade
Brig. D. Dawnay, DSO, Commanding
1st North Irish Horse
12th Battalion Royal Tank Regiment
48th Battalion Royal Tank Regiment
17th Indian Infantry Brigade
Brig. P. R. MacMamara, DSO,
Commanding
1st Battalion The Royal Fusiliers
(City of London Regiment)
1st Battalion 12th Frontier Force
Regiment
1st Battalion 5th Royal Ghurka Rifles
19th Indian Infantry Brigade
Brig. T. S. Dobree, DSO, MC,
Commanding
1st Battalion The Argyll and Sutherland
Highlanders (Princess Louise's)
3rd Battalion 8th Punjab Regiment
6th Royal Battalion 13th Frontier Force
Rifles
21st Indian Infantry Brigade

Brig. B. S. Mould, DSO, OBE, MC,
Commanding
5th Battalion The Queen's Own Royal
West Kent Regiment
1st Battalion 5th Mahrattas
3rd Battalion 15th Punjab Regiment

56TH INFANTRY DIVISION
Maj. Gen. J. Y. Whitfield, DSO, OBE,
Commanding

78TH INFANTRY DIVISION
Brig. R. K. Arbuthnott, DSO, MC,
Commanding

CREMONA COMBAT GROUP (Italian)
Maj. Gen. Primieri, Commanding

X CORPS
Lt. Gen. J. L. I. Hawksworth, CB, CBE, DSO,
Commanding

X CORPS TROOPS
Royal Artillery
Brig. M. N. Dewing, CBE, DSO, MC,
Artillery Officer
2nd Regiment Royal Horse Artillery
200th Field Regiment
75th Medium Regiment
57th Anti-Tank Regiment
1st Heavy Anti-Aircraft Regiment
(one battery)
567th Searchlight Battery (one troop)
655th Air OP Squadron (one flight)
Royal Engineers
Brig. E. V. Daldy, Chief Engineer
X Corps Troops Royal Engineers
242nd Field Company
558th Field Company
258th Corps Field Park Company
8th Battalion The Royal Fusiliers
(City of London Regiment)

JEWISH INFANTRY BRIGADE GROUP
Brig. E. F. Benjamin, Commanding

FRIULI COMBAT GROUP
General Scattini, Commanding

XIII CORPS
Lt. Gen. Sir John Harding, KCB, CBE, DSO,
MC, Commanding

XIII CORPS TROOPS
Royal Artillery
  Brig. H. Greene, CBE, MC, Artillery
  Officer
    3rd Survey Regiment
    655th Air OP Squadron (less one flight)
    57th Field Regiment (one battery and
      one troop)
6th Army Group Royal Artillery
  Brig. J. St. C. Holbrook, CBE, MC,
  Commanding
    66th Medium Regiment (4.5-inch)
    75th Heavy Regiment (Mixed)
      (two sections)
    126th Meteorological Section
2nd Anti-Aircraft Brigade
  Brig. H. M. MacIntyre, CBE, DSO,
  Commanding
    1st Heavy Anti-Aircraft Regiment
      (less one battery)
    51st Heavy Anti-Aircraft Regiment
    11th Light Anti-Aircraft Regiment
    51st Light Anti-Aircraft Regiment
    53rd Light Anti-Aircraft Regiment
      (less one battery)
    47th Anti-Aircraft Operations Room
Royal Engineers
  Brig. J. C. Walkey, OBE, Chief Engineer
    XIII Corps Troops Royal Engineers
    56th Field Company
    577th Army Field Company
    578th Army Field Company
    576th Corps Field Park Company

10TH INDIAN INFANTRY DIVISION
Maj. Gen. D. W. Reid, CBE, DSO, MC,
Commanding
  10th Indian Division Artillery
  Brig. W. R. Goodeman, MC,
  Commanding

FOLGORE COMBAT GROUP (Italian)
Maj. Gen. Morigi, Commanding

2 POLISH CORPS
Lt. Gen. W. Anders, Commanding
Maj. Gen. Z. Bohusz-Szyszko, Deputy
Commander

2 POLISH CORPS TROOPS
Artillery
  Maj. Gen. R. Odierzynski, Artillery
  Officer
    1st Polish Survey Regiment
    7th Polish Anti-Tank Regiment
      (less one battery)
    663rd Polish Air OP Squadron
    567th Searchlight Battery
      (less one troop)
    8th Polish Heavy Anti-Aircraft Artillery
      (one battery)
Army Group Polish Artillery
  Col. K. Zabkowski, Commanding
    10th Polish Medium Regiment (5.5-inch)
    11th Polish Medium Regiment (4.5-inch)
    12th Polish Medium Regiment (4.5-inch)
    13th Polish Medium Regiment (5.5-inch)
    78th Medium Regiment (5.5-inch)
    9th Polish Heavy Regiment (Mixed)
Headquarters 2nd Polish Corps Troops Polish
Engineers
  Col. J. Sochocki, Commanding
    4th Carpathian Rifle Battalion
    5th Carpathian Rifle Battalion
    6th Carpathian Rifle Battalion
3rd Carpathian Rifle Brigade
  Lt. Col. G. Lowczowski, Commanding
    7th Carpathian Rifle Battalion
    8th Carpathian Rifle Battalion
    9th Carpathian Rifle Battalion

5TH KRESOWA INFANTRY DIVISION
Maj. Gen. Sulik, Commanding
  Artillery

Index

Compiled by Lori L. Daniel